W9-COI-938

U.S.A. Antiques
12905 Main Street
Rogers, MN 55374
763-428-0101

GENERAL STORE

COLLECTIBLES

IDENTIFICATION & VALUE GUIDE

Volume
II

David L. Wilson

COLLECTOR BOOKS

A Division of Schroeder Publishing Co., Inc.

The current values in this book should be used only as a guide. They are not intended to set prices, which vary from one section of the country to another. Auction prices as well as dealer prices vary greatly and are affected by condition as well as demand. Neither the Author nor the Publisher assumes responsibility for any losses that might be incurred as a result of consulting this guide.

Searching For A Publisher?

We are always looking for knowledgeable people considered to be experts within their fields. If you feel that there is a real need for a book on your collectible subject and have a large comprehensive collection, contact Collector Books.

On the Cover:

1. Pumpkin tin with boy holding pumpkin. Paper label. $28.00 – 55.00. Wilson Collection.

2. Large Enterprise coffee grinder Model #18. $3,200.00 – 4,500.00. Courtesy of Harvey Leventhal.

3. Security Stock Powder box, Security Remedy Co., original contents. $150.00 – 250.00. Courtesy of Ken Kennedy.

4. Dr. A.C. Daniels Lotion, original contents. $50.00 – 100.00. Wilson Collection.

5. Summer Girl Black Pepper. $225.00 – 350.00. Courtesy of Ken Kennedy.

6. Tiger Chewing Tobacco store canisters. Orange, $175.00 – 325.00; blue, $425.00 – 750.00.

7. Country Merchant 5¢ cigar, large fabric banner. $2,500.00 – 3,200.00. Wilson Collection.

Cover Design: Beth Summers

Book Design: Benjamin R. Faust

COLLECTOR BOOKS
P.O. Box 3009
Paducah, KY 42002-3009

Copyright © 1998 by David L. Wilson

All rights reserved. No part of this book may be reproduced, stored in any retrieval system, or transmitted in any form, or by any means including but not limited to electronic, mechanical, photocopy, recording, or otherwise, without the written consent of the author and publisher.

⋆❖ CONTENTS ❖⋆

·✦ DEDICATION ✦·

To my daughter
  Amanda Jean Wilson

And to my sons
  Grant Spencer Wilson and Shane David Wilson

Being a collector and American history enthusiast can be a real challenge when kids are involved. As I clearly recall, a toy store or an amusement park was much more to my liking as a child than antique shops and museums. My children were no different.

Their protests were considered and, on most trips, I tried to include them in an activity of their interest. I thank them for joining me on countless visits to old country stores, antique shops, historical sites, museums, and homes of collectors. Our trips covered states from California to Maine. Old homesteads in Kansas and ghost towns high in the mountains of Colorado were frequent destinations.

Some of the antique shows included more than 1,000 dealers and turned out to be all-day affairs. My heartfelt thanks to you dealers that shared stories, candy, toys, and other treats with my kids. It certainly confirms my feeling that antique dealers are among some of the very finest folks out there.

There was a time when I held Amanda in one arm and Grant in the other as we walked from shop to shop. One of our favorite shops was Vince Harbick's Smockville Station Antiques in Sherwood, Oregon. Vince always seemed to have some cookies or candy for well-behaved children. Shane became so knowledgeable about my interests that he would frequently spot a tobacco tin or advertising item and quickly bring it to my attention.

Shane, Amanda, and Grant, thanks for all the special joys you add to my life. The father in me loves each of you more than I can say, and the collector in me is thankful for all the times we spent together on the collector's trail. God bless you always!

⋯⊹ ABOUT THE AUTHOR ⊹⋯

David Wilson has been an avid country store collector for more than 25 years and his enthusiasm for the golden age of the old mercantile store continues to grow. He has been an antique dealer and appraiser and also operated a general store museum at California's Gold Discovery site, Coloma.

He is a student of American history and enjoys talking with groups and organizations about America's past. He has completed extensive research about the old-time country store and has had the opportunity to talk with numbers of people that had a sharp recall of the general store and what it was really like.

Wilson has lived in the states of Ohio, Missouri, Washington, California, Arizona, Colorado, Montana, and Oregon. His travels have provided the opportunity to visit countless museums, historical sites, and early stores and talk with "old-timers" about the good old days.

He is a member of the Antique Advertising Association of America, Tins and Signs, Oregon State Historical Society, and the Clackamas County Historical Society. He has written numerous articles and is the author of *General Store Collectibles Volume 1* and *Great American West Collectibles*.

He resides in Wilsonville, Oregon, with his wife, Cindy, and their two children, Amanda and Grant.

COUNTRY STORE

It filled the corner where the crossroads meet;
A hitching rail once stood beside the door,
The old potbellied stove to warm the feet,
A black coal hod to keep the trash from the floor.

Here the neighbors used to gather every night;
They sat on sturdy chairs with tilted legs.
Here every man could feed his appetite
For news and wait for sorting of his eggs.

This was the meeting place of countrymen;
They waded mud or plowed through the winter snow
To purchase from the stock they offered then
Of flour, nails, and bright-sprigged calico.

The store is gone, but I recall the time
When I could buy all heaven for a dime.

Helen Virden

The time is just after the turn of the century. The place is Lipper Brothers General Merchandise store in Rago, Kansas. The clerk is taking an order from a young boy who has been sent to the store by his mother. The anxious boy reads the note, "A pound of American cheese, a bottle of vanilla an' half a peck of sweet p'taters an' a pound of graham crackers an'a pound of brown sugar an' a pound of butter — an' Ma says I can spend th' rest of th' dollar for lickrish an' jelly beans."

One storekeeper once had a problem with a lady who would steal cheese at every opportunity, but was otherwise a good customer. He gave some thought to the case of the cheese-swiping old woman and soon developed a plan. The stock of cheeses included a very firm cheese of light yellow color. Goodwill Soap was very similar in appearance. The storekeeper took a bar of Goodwill Soap, cut out a wedge of it, and substituted the soap wedge in the wheel of cheese. As expected, the customer helped herself while the storekeeper was occupied with another customer. Gagging and sputtering, she hid behind some dry goods until her coughing spasm passed. Finally she came out, paid for a purchase, and was never seen in that store again.

In 1900 there were probably more than 20,000 brands of chewing and smoking tobacco for "chaws," snuff, pipes, cigars, and cigarettes. This explains the wealth of tobacco-related collectibles.

"Store-bought" or "store-boughten" was once a proud phrase, meaning the possessor of the item had modern taste and "cash money." There were two criteria for anything so described: It had to be a manufactured product and purchased at retail price.

Western storekeeping in Kansas, Iowa, and Missouri Territories was not for the faint hearted. Many hopefully loaded their stores, complete with assorted braids, buttons, edgings and trimmings, in a covered wagon, crossed miles of difficult country and ferried over the Mississippi, took one look at the wide and empty country, and turned their horses back toward the green hills of home.

Use Kohler One Night Corn Cure. Illustrates a man attempting to remove corns the old fashioned way — with a straight razor. Heavy paperboard ad. So typical of an ad that would have been used in an early general store. Circa 1900. $95.00 – 135.00. Wilson Collection

❖ ACKNOWLEDGMENTS ❖

I could write a volume thanking all those that have shared their knowledge with me and helped make collecting such a truly incredible pastime. I look over the past 30 years and can recall so many wonderful people.

As I mentioned in my first book, Chuck and Jennie Melville of Paradise, California, opened my eyes to the joy of collecting old store items and advertising. They continue to offer fine merchandise at fair prices. I'm always happy to see them at the Portland Expo Shows. Yes, I'm still purchasing items from them. Chuck always has some interesting stories and at the July 1997 show, Jennie had some candy treats for Amanda and Grant.

Very special thanks to Ken Kennedy of Seattle, Washington; Larry Manos of Buffalo Bay Auction Company in Rogers, Minnesota; and Harvey Leventhal of Ellwood City, Pennsylvania. All of these fine gentlemen were very kind to share photographs of outstanding country store collectibles.

Many other dealers and collectors come to mind. Peter Lovejoy, who does business as The Blue Tiger and lives in the beautiful state of New Hampshire, is always a welcome sight at a show. Everything in his booth is first-class as attested by my shrinking wallet after our initial meeting. I have purchased some of my real "treasures" from Peter and had some very pleasant and informative conversations with him.

Dan Weaver of Main Street Antiques in Independence, Oregon, has one of those shops that is becoming more difficult to find these days with quality merchandise and always a friendly welcome. Independence, Oregon, is a very historic town that retains much of its 1890 flavor. Dan's shop is something to behold.

Thanks to Robert Harper of Cary Station Antiques in Cary, Illinois; Ron Schieber of Mad Money in Akron, Ohio; David Hirsch of Morton Grove, Illinois; Myron Huffman of Hoagland, Indiana; Phil and Karol Atkinson of Mercer, Pennsylvania; Tom Killeen of Webster Groves, Missouri; Bob Brunswick of Buggy Step Antiques in Peninsula, Ohio; and John and Mary Jo Purdum of Cheap John's Country Store in Waynesville, Ohio.

A warm thanks to my lovely wife, Cindy, who was always available to bounce ideas off and offer encouragement.

To all of you who purchased *General Store Collectibles* and made it the best-selling book on the subject, thank you. For those of you who called me and sent kind letters, I truly appreciated hearing from you.

A NOTE ON PRICING

As I pointed out in my first book, determining a fair market value for general store collectibles is a difficult task.

So many factors can influence values at any given time. Economic conditions, supply and demand, condition, scarcity, the personal motivation of buyers and sellers, and regional variances all can enter into the equation.

It is recommended that the collector talk with other reputable collectors and dealers as much as possible to keep in touch with the market.

A price guide is just that — a guide. Advertising and store collectibles from the 1870 to 1930 period are in limited supply. Prices can vary considerably. The enthusiasm of a collector to acquire an item can lead to a selling price that is "off the chart."

My effort is to provide the collector, dealer, and enthusiast with value information that has been culled from a number of sources. Those sources include my personal knowledge as a long-time collector; reported auction prices; discussions with collectors and dealers throughout the United States; following trade journals; frequent visits to antique shops; and attending numerous collectors' shows.

The ultimate price is established by what a buyer is willing to pay. I anticipate the market will fluctuate as most markets do. If the number of collectors for old store memorabilia continues to grow, the market remains stable, and the demand is strong, one can expect prices to advance. On the other hand, thousands of collectors are now focused on collectibles from the 1940s, '50s, '60s, and even '70s. Prices are generally lower for this 40-year period and the collectibles are within the memory of the collectors. In talking with young collectors, I find many that are reluctant to focus on old store and advertising primarily as a result of the price ranges. Time will tell us what eventual impact this will have.

In the meantime, I feel collectibles of the old general store have significant historical and art form value. Advertising posters, tobacco and coffee tins, coffee grinders, store fixtures, ornate cash registers, early boxed games and trade cards, to name a few, are among some of the most desirable collectibles available. I know that my enthusiasm is just as strong as always!

⊷ INTRODUCTION ⊷

This book continues to chronicle the era of the old country store in America and the living heritage of collectibles that were once found within its walls.

In my previous book, *General Store Collectibles,* I focused on a variety of items and subjects that will not be found in this book. Volume 1 featured patent medicines, cash registers, Christmas at the general store, dye cupboards, and vet cabinets, to name a few. There was also a chapter on care and restoration.

Volume 2 brings forth a completely different array of fascinating collectibles along with historical perspectives of the important role of the general store in the "good old days." It is, I hope, an attempt to capture through words and photos the wonderful nostalgia of an institution that contributed substantially to the development of our nation.

It was indeed a remarkable era, made even more remarkable by the fact that countless numbers of memorabilia have survived to provide vivid reminders of a period that has vanished. There will soon come a time, as it always does, when no living person will have a first-hand account of what the old general stores were truly like. I have always enjoyed talking with people who have sharp recollections and fond memories of their visits to the store. It was something to anticipate and generally was a very pleasant experience.

To hold a tobacco tin or view a lithographed advertising sign that was once held or viewed by unknown persons in the era of roughly 1870 to 1920 represents a clear path to our past. Reading store ledgers, letters, and billheads certainly brings history alive. How many hands, for example, has a circa 1900 coffee tin passed through to reach today's collecting market? One can only ponder.

Where else but the old country store could a child walk through the door and expect to find a penny's worth of licorice or a wide variety of other delicious candies at modest prices?

As most collectors and enthusiasts are aware, the largest number of available items from the store era date after 1900. From time to time, a collector will have the opportunity to acquire an item from as early as 1870, but such items are scarce and not usually in good condition.

This book is directed to collectors, potential collectors, enthusiasts, and any person with strong interests in America's fascinating heritage.

Collecting old store items continues to grow in popularity and many pleasant times and exciting discoveries are waiting. Enjoy every moment!

Chapter One
··❖ THE HISTORIC GENERAL STORE ❖··

The roots of the historic general store remain strong. Throughout America, you can still find stores that have been in the same location since the nineteenth century. The floorboards still creak, hard candies that taste like root beer are still available, and there may even be some handmade brooms and ceramic crocks. Many carry items that are just as appealing today as they were 100 years ago. A very popular restaurant chain, Cracker Barrel Country Stores, has found success in reaching back to another century and utilizing the spirit of the old store culture.

I have always enjoyed trips to Vermont. In addition to the fabulous scenery, friendly folks, and quaint villages, there is a pleasing abundance of country stores. If you have never had an opportunity to visit Vermont and you are an old-store enthusiast, you should not miss it!

Where else can you find multitudes of country stores that offer trout flies, boots, nails, shotgun shells, homemade pie, penny candies, spirited conversation, and directions? In Vermont, the general store represents a way of life and Vermonters are fighting hard to protect and perpetuate it. There are even $3,500.00 grants available to selected stores for improvements.

Just as in the nineteenth century, people gather at general stores in Vermont and other states to discuss the issues of the day. Some of the stores in Vermont have been in the same family for more than 100 years.

Certainly an institution that has survived for so many years is very special.

There is a hero in the pages of American history that has not been recognized. When the Eastern part of the United States was a frontier, he was there. He traveled west as the country expanded. At great peril to himself and his family and with bright optimism for the future, he invested in a stock of goods and joined throngs of others on the overland trails.

A collection of crude dwellings could become an honest-to-God settlement with his presence. The old-time storekeeper helped provide the necessities of life as well as some luxuries. He gave his customers a place to barter their goods — everything from hides and eggs to feathers. What other person frequently provided the multiple roles of local official, post office operator, insurance agent, banker, trader, and someone who could help with contracts and other documents?

His ability to understand the needs of the local population as well as their problems was often without peer. Going to the store for a bit of trading, conversation, or learning about happenings in the community was a welcome diversion from the rigors and stresses of the day. It is more than coincidental that when you read the historical remembrances of people that lived in the glory years of the old country store, they often recall with great fondness the store of their memories.

Yes, the old-time storekeeper, his wife, and family were vital to those they served. Labor being what it was in the nineteenth and early twentieth centuries, the storekeeper had to count on the contributions of his family to survive and prosper. His knowledge of trading had to be keen. His selection of goods required a very personal knowledge of those who visited his store. Most were a buggy ride away from the store and were well known. If the stock was not selected carefully and the profit margin considered in detail, store inventory would not sell and profits would be elusive at best.

If one truly considers the complex nature and abilities required to be a successful storekeeper from roughly 1800 to 1930, it would be a position that most would not apply for. Mostly forgotten by 1930, much as the country doctor, the general storekeeper passed from the scene without much acclaim. I'm hopeful that somewhere in our grand land there is a monument to a storekeeper, but I've yet to find one.

Dogs, sea gulls, outlaws, and questionable politicians have received monuments of various sorts, but what of the old-time storekeeper?

The crossroads country store and its town cousin, the general store, were outstanding examples of free enterprise in action. Every store was unique by location, goods carried, character of the proprietor, and clientele served. A store in a sparsely settled area of Nebraska may have had limited goods with little variety. On the other hand, a thriving general store of the 1880s in a booming Kansas cow town could be expected to carry everything from factory-made clothes to an unending variety of fancy goods. No two stores were ever alike, right down to the smell. Spices from the Orient, strong tobaccos, saddles, harness goods, coffee, tea, coal oil, toys at Christmas, and other stock all mingled together to provide unique and generally welcome smells.

In 1960, a gentleman who was born at the time of the Civil War was asked what reminded him most of the old days. He commented that the "honest to God smell of an old general store" could do just that.

Stores could be open from 6:00 in the morning until 10:00 at night. Customers relied on the store being open and showed up when it was necessary or convenient. As a practical utility and a convenience to customers, a large number of storekeepers lived in rooms above the store. Needless to say, demanding folks often interrupted slumber. Medicines for man and beast, a wagon part, whiskey, tobacco, and ammunition were frequently requested at late hours.

One of the classic happenings in a general store was the conversation, or lack of it. A story was told about a storekeeper in Kansas that was found talking to himself as a countryman entered the store. When asked why he was talking to himself, the proprietor curtly commented that he had been looking for an interesting person to talk to all day and, "Thank God had found one!"

Views were often exchanged on a variety of subjects including politics, religion, the price of farm goods, and the various qualities of a specific horse. When strong disagreements occurred, the storekeeper was often the only source of maintaining the peace. The proprietor was looked to as the arbitrator, and his views were generally respected. After all, it was within his power to grant or deny credit, or influence a person's standing in the community in more subtle ways.

Much like today's retail world, there were often instances of intense competition among the general stores of yesteryear. In 1884, a small town in Oregon had three general stores. The local market would only support one so the rivalry was hot and furious. Prices were discounted. Free gifts were given with purchases, and loyalty was demanded. Finally, the owners of two of the stores got together and decided to join forces and have one large store, thereby eliminating the competition. Sound familiar? In spite of this merger, the community decided to support the smaller general store and the two partners eventually moved to another town to avoid ruin. A resident later commented that "gangin' up wern't fair."

A time finally came when many general stores offered home delivery. The merchant equipped the store with a wagon or two, depending on the volume of business, and had his store name prominently displayed. My collection contains a postal card from 1902 that was sent to a general store in Ohio with the following request, "When your delivery wagon comes up our way, please send us 1# Butter; 1# Good quality cheese; 1# Soda Biscuit; ½# Tea; 2oz. Allspice; ½ gal. Coal Oil; 1 Bitters Tonic." The request was signed by George C. Weimer, 839 Dayton St., City.

It is extremely interesting to review correspondence that was sent by a general store owner in the operation of his business. I have a number of such letters in my collection and they provide a wonderful glimpse of the trials and tribulations of keeping store.

There are letters concerning disputes about the quality of crackers sent by a supplier; the problems experienced in hiring honest clerks willing to work long hours; efforts made to collect bad debts; decisions regarding which drummers to deal with and those to avoid; and, most importantly, how to increase profits.

Many general stores had posted rules which appear very harsh by today's more liberal standards. A representative set of popular store rules follows:

☛ Store must be promptly opened at 6:00 a.m. and remain open until 9 p.m. the year round.

☛ Store must not be opened on the Sabbath Day unless absolutely necessary and then only for a few minutes.

☛ Any employee who is in the habit of smoking Spanish cigarettes, getting shaved at a barber shop, going to dances and such places of amusement, will most surely give his employer reason to be suspicious of his integrity and all around honesty.

☛ Each employee must pay not less than $5.00 per year to the church and must attend Sunday School every Sunday.

☛ Men employees are given one evening a week for courting purposes and two if they go to prayer meeting regularly.

☛ Leisure time must be spent in reading good literature.

The general store served a vital spot in the development and progression of America. Its heritage will remain with us always.

The caption on the back of this photo reads, "New store after fire of 1908 — Meek Mercantile Company, Comptonville, California." Just the kind of store a collector would love to visit if only we could turn back the clock. Notice the corset display, scale, family sitting on the stools, hanging brass lamps, and the wonderful variety of merchandise. $35.00 – 50.00. Wilson Collection

The writing on the back of this photo states, "Store in Jefferson." No identity on the state. Here we see hanging bananas and brooms with a large coffee grinder on the counter. There is a phone at the rear of the store just below an ad for flour. This store offers a large inventory of canned goods. $30.00 – 45.00. Wilson Collection

A fine photo of a store with a large merchandiser counter with a fancy brass cash register. There is a yeast ad to the rear of the store on the right side. The store clerk is anxious for customers. $30.00 – 45.00. Wilson Collection

Fresh baked bread, Newmark's Coffee, Snider's catsup, Holsum bread, Washington state apples, and Mama's Cookies are just a few of the attractions in this store. There is a large merchandiser counter with windows at the rear of the store. This store had joined the electric age. $30.00 – 45.00. Wilson Collection

The hardware section of a very large general store. The store offers a wide variety of stoves including top-of-the-line cook stoves with warming ovens. Notice the large die cut ad of the old gentleman at the right rear of the store. All hardware needs could be met in this establishment. $25.00 – 35.00. Wilson Collection

Lipper Bros. General Merchandise Store in Rago, Kansas. As often was the case, this store also housed the post office. Coal and grain were some of the needs of the day. Notice the hitching posts, milk container, pump, chickens, and clothing ad in the right window. A great exterior photo. $35.00 – 50.00. Wilson Collection

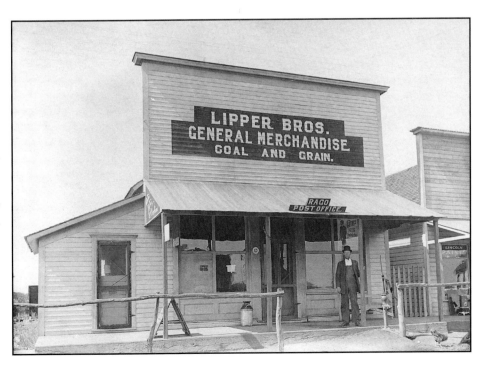

A wonderful photo. This general store offers a wide selection of goods. Hats, shoes, seeds, crackers, fancy men's shirts, and fresh fruit are just a few of the items available. The back of the photo is stamped "Norfolk, Nebraska." $40.00 – 60.00. Wilson Collection

Signs are hanging from the ceiling advertising Lava Soap and Davis Baking powder. Notice the four gentlemen enjoying some refreshment on the left side of the store. A large number of glass showcases on the right permit easy view of the merchandise. The merchant also has the advantage of some organization. One can only speculate about the conversation that must have been going on. The photo is marked "North Vernon, Illinois." $40.00 – 60.00. Wilson Collection

A great photo of a general store in Nebraska. There is an extensive post office section but not a great deal of merchandise present. The gentleman is standing next to a poster advertising a carnival at Redfield, South Dakota. Enticements include bands of music, a great ferris wheel, and cash carnival midway shows. There is a lithographed Rice's seed box on the right and ads for Nic Nac Tobacco and James G. Blaine 5-Cent Cigars are posted. Fresh shrimp is also available along with money orders. $45.00 – 70.00. Wilson Collection

This store presents a very prosperous appearance. The merchant has a wide variety of goods available. Kellogg's Toasted Corn Flakes; Ferry & Co. Seeds; Fairbanks Sunny Monday Laundry Soap; Cottolene, which is advertised as containing "no hog fat" and "best for shortening and frying;" and Pioneer Brand Sea Clams are just a few of the products offered in this attractive store. $40.00 – 60.00. Wilson Collection

Boxes of boots and shoes, a bench for weary customers, and an ornate stove greet customers of this store. Ribbon and spool cases are displayed in the dry goods section. Could the well-dressed gentleman leaning on the showcase be a drummer? He appears to be holding an advertisement. $40.00 – 60.00. Wilson Collection

This store is proud to offer cold storage. Butter and eggs are available. There is a large display of National Biscuit Company products in their individual bins. Old Dutch Cleanser, Argo Starch, Ohio Blue Tip Matches, Baronet Biscuits, Imperial Cigarettes, Koko 5-Cent Grab Box, and fresh bread are among the offerings to customers. $35.00 – 45.00. Wilson Collection

The inscription on the back of the photo indicates that this is "Harris Hughes father's store." No other identification. This is another store that gives every appearance of prosperity. Extensive stock that is well-displayed and eager clerks add up to a thriving business. Just above the store clerk that is completing the wrapping of a purchase is an incredible string holder. The product advertised is Swift's Pride Washing Powder and shows a pretty girl holding the string with her right arm and resting her left arm on the side of the product. $40.00 – 65.00. Wilson Collection

A photo of the 1940 era. The storekeeper could easily have been in an early 1900s setting given his appearance. Such stores were diminishing in number at that time but were still active in rural America. $30.00 – 45.00. Wilson Collection

A print of an American Country Store illustrating the 1850 – 1860 period. Notice there are no packaged goods and a large stock of fabric materials for making clothing. This store maintained the local post office and would have bartered for produce and other goods brought in by customers. Two dogs and a cat are present to enliven the day. Several of the men folk are "holding court" around the stove, swapping news and, perhaps, some outlandish stories. The print was made around 1900. $12.00 – 20.00. Wilson Collection

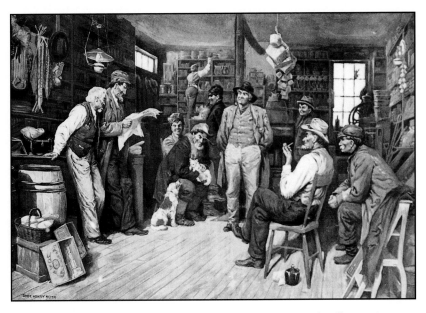

An early print entitled "A Market Report, Corn Is Up." The illustration was done by Robert Henry Roth. The print is dated 1903. A very fine print showing a busy and important day at the general store. $200.00 – 350.00. Courtesy of The Vermont Country Store

D. C. Heuer's General Store, Bergholz, New York. Mr. and Mrs. Heuer and family are pictured in front. Note the living quarters attached to the store. $35.00 – 50.00. Courtesy of Ann Heuer

A Perfection Coffee container, prepared for D. C. Heuer's General Store, Berholz, New York. Circa 1915. $30.00 – 42.00. Courtesy of Ann Heuer

Wonderful early interior photograph of a well-stocked general store. The caption on the back of the photo identifies the location as Plainview, Texas, and is dated 1905. "Auntee's and Uncle Lee's store" also inscribed on the back. Large sign at the rear of the store warns "PLEASE DO NOT ASK FOR CREDIT." Notice the very long merchandiser counter on the right. This store offers a large variety of canned goods. $45.00 – 70.00. Wilson Collection

A store of the 1920 – 1930 period. There is a candlestick phone behind the counter ready to take orders. Advertising for numerous products. A good supply of Bishop's Crackers is on hand. $25.00 – 35.00. Courtesy of Peter Crandell

A classic country store, circa 1890 – 1910. The store features custom-made counters with several showcases of various sizes. Advertising for Ferry Seeds, Pearline Soap, and KC Baking Powder. A selection of fresh meat is offered at the rear of the store. $35.00 – 50.00. Wilson Collection

Chapter Two
⟡ STORE FIXTURES ⟡

The era of the old general store provided a wide departure from what we are accustomed to as we approach the twenty-first century. Today's chain super-markets and national variety stores generally look the same in Seattle, Boston, and other locations.

A traveler in the late nineteenth and early twen-tieth centuries would have found only unique stores which tended to characterize the merchant's idea of what a store's interior should look like. Established stores often boasted custom counters and shelving that could be very elaborate. In contrast, stores in developing farming and mining areas frequently uti-lized rough lumber. The important thing was to open for business quickly in such areas and receive some financial return. I have some photos in my collection that show the use of tents and crude canvas struc-tures in establishing the first general stores in newly-founded town sites.

A general store in the early days of the mining camp of Tincup, Colorado, shows an interior crammed with goods with no effort made to bring organization to the situation. The storekeeper was often faced with a problem locating a requested item. Display cases were non-existent so store inventory could often be misplaced. On the other hand, the local mercantile store in Bellows Falls, Vermont, exhibits a strong sense of order and tidiness. A cus-tomer in such a store expected the merchant to be able instantly to locate a requested item.

Open barrels, boxes, and bins that contained bulk goods were placed in various locations throughout a store. Orders were given to the merchant or his clerk who proceeded to gather the requested items while the customer waited and perhaps engaged in some conversation.

A large two-wheeled coffee grinder and a tobacco plug cutter were two fixtures that could be found in all early stores. The storekeeper would acquire fix-tures that suited him which he felt to be necessary.

Display cases were particularly welcome if they came free of charge. In exchange, the company providing the display case insisted that only their products be placed in the case. Many came with the product name etched in the glass of the display case. The cases made a product stand out in the overall confusion.

Display cases and cupboards for such diverse products as Diamond Dyes, scissors, and knives, silk and thread, ammunition, firearms, inks, livestock remedies, garters, gents' collars, and patent medi-cines all found their way into general stores.

Stoves were placed in different locations. If the storekeeper was fond of the gossip and the checker playing that went on around the store stove during the winter months, the stove might be placed in the middle of the store. Its location represented an informal meeting and lounging area and was very popular.

If the storekeeper was "all business," he might prefer to see his stove at the rear of the store where "riff-raff" would not interfere with more desirable customers. Loud-talking men could often intimidate the less vocal customer.

A clear sign of prosperity was the presence of a fancy brass cash register. The "tingle" of the regis-ter's bell was welcome music to the storekeeper and, hopefully, a device that encouraged sales.

"Honest weight" scales were necessary and it was possible for a store to have a variety of scales. Depending on region, there could have been a need for gold scales. Additionally, scales for weighing everything from candy to hardware were present. Many babies had their first weighing recorded at the general store.

Some storekeepers made every effort to utilize all the space available, including hanging a multitude of goods from the ceiling.

It was possible to find elaborate offices in some stores with the bottom range being simply a wooden box containing bills, invoices, and other documents. Roll-top desks were in favor due to multiple storage areas and small compartments. Also, such desks could be easily locked and private matters secured.

Some customers visited the general store so frequently that they had a better idea of the inventory than did the proprietor.

One of the truly enjoyable store memorabilia that I collect is original photos illustrating the interiors of American general stores. The interiors are remarkable in their own right but no two are ever alike and all of them make a statement of some sort. I made certain to include a number of them in both of my books.

When you examine them closely with a strong magnifying glass, you can clearly see that each store has a very special look. From the extent of the merchandise to the manner in which store fixtures are used, each store was one of a kind.

Storekeepers exhibited strong pride in their mercantile businesses and generally always found a place for a new store fixture that advertised a particular product or products. A brightly colored black and orange hanging lamp advertising None Such mincemeat, ceiling string holders, bag holders, broom holders, whip holders, gun cabinets, nail and bolt cabinets, and coffee bins were all eagerly accepted from manufacturers and distributors. These items are now among the most sought after store collectibles.

Merrick's Spool Cotton oak cabinet. $1,850.00 – 2,600.00.

Adams Pepsin/Tutti Frutti display cabinet. $675.00 – 800.00.

Putnam Fadeless Dyes. Wood-framed cabinet. Monroe Drug Co., Quincy, Illinois. $225.00 – 375.00.

Large postal unit. $2,250.00 – 3,200.00.

Wall phone. Oak case. $265.00 – 350.00.

Fairbanks scale. $225.00 – 275.00.

Very scarce seed dispenser. Jesse Lines Seed Cabinet. Sabetha, Kansas. $2,650.00 – 3,200.00.

Oak ribbon case. $425.00 – 750.00.

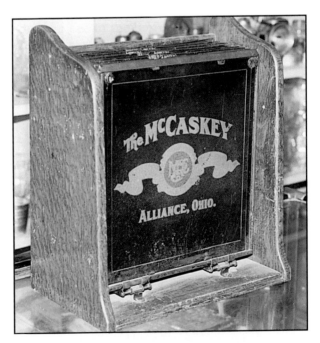

Large counter scale. The Computing Scale Co., Dayton, Ohio. $375.00 – 525.00.

Account ledger case with swinging metal partitions. The McCaskey, Alliance, Ohio. $350.00 – 500.00.

Small oak-framed display case. Very desirable size. Used for displaying personal items. $275.00 – 400.00.

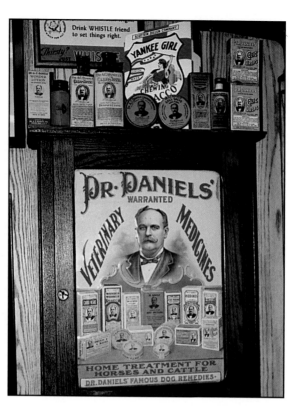

Dr. Daniels Veterinary Medicines store cabinet. This one is particularly unusual. It contains the original products. There are also some displayed on the top of the cabinet. $2,400.00 – 3,500.00.
Courtesy Peter Crandall

Another variety of a beautiful Merrick's Spool cabinet. Very fine condition. $1,850.00 – $2,600.00.

Hanging brass store lamp. $225.00 – 375.00.

Store cheese case with revolving wheel. $325.00 – 525.00.

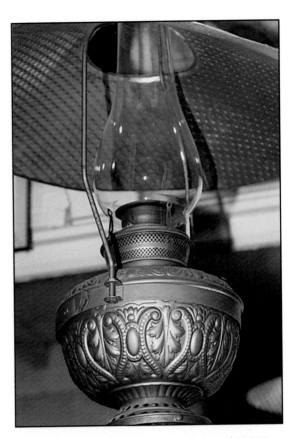

Hanging embossed brass store lamp. $225.00 – 375.00.

Dayton counter scale. Green with gold bands. The customer could observe the "honest weight" through the glass display area. $425.00 – 650.00. Wilson Collection

A large Richardson's Spool Silk oak cabinet. $1,000.00 – 1,500.00. Courtesy Harvey Leventhal

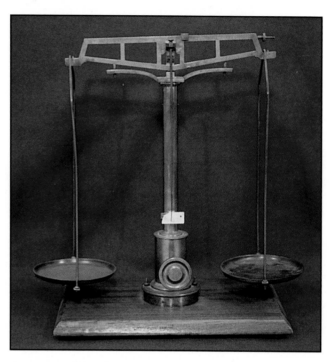

Counter gold scales. General stores in the American West in the early days frequently traded in gold dust and nuggets. $450.00 – 700.00. *Wilson Collection*

National Coffee Mill, Elgin, Illinois. $725.00 – 900.00.

Hunt's Round Pointed pen case containing an assortment. Also, a very interesting large metal advertising pen point. Case, $425.00 – 750; Point, $175.00 – 300.00.

A very unusual oak store case with lower bins, drawers, and a variety of upper compartments. $3,200.00 – 4,800.00.

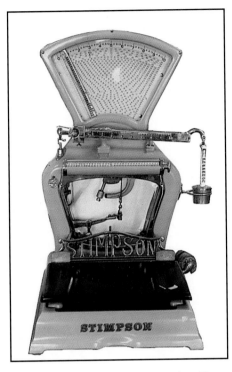

Stimpson scale. Very nice detailing.
$750.00 – 900.00. Courtesy of Buffalo Bay
Auction Co.

Barler's Ideal Oil Heat stove. This stove
was a welcome replacement for the wood
burning stoves. $375.00 – 485.00.

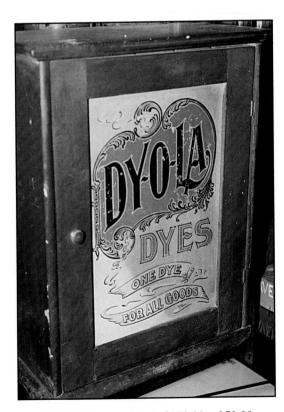

Apothecary scale. Some storekeepers also dispensed
drugs. $250.00 – 375.00.

DY-O-LA Dyes cabinet. $240.00 – 350.00.

Oak framed Slidewell Collar case. $800.00 – 1,200.00. Courtesy of Harvey Leventhal

Oak money order unit with frosted glass window. $650.00 – 900.00.

Utz & Dunn Co. standing advertising sign for Ladies and Misses Footwear, Rochester, N.Y. Reverse on glass, mirror on reverse. Floor stand. $1,000.00 – 1,400.00. Courtesy of Buffalo Bay Auction Co.

National Cash Register with the name of the firm, Nelson & Co., on the front brass plate. This was generally an "extra cost" item. $700.00 – 900.00. Courtesy Buffalo Bay Auction Co.

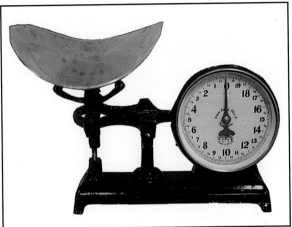

*Penn counter scale with brass hopper. $150.00 –
250.00. Courtesy Buffalo Bay Auction Co.*

*Belding's Silk/Spool Silk oak cabinet. $800.00 –
1,000.00. Courtesy Buffalo Bay Auction Co.*

*Iron string holder with twine. $145.00 –
185.00. Courtesy Buffalo Bay Auction Co.*

Riverside Oak store stove. $375.00 – 650.00.

Unusual tobacco display case. $300.00 – 500.00. Courtesy of Harvey Leventhal

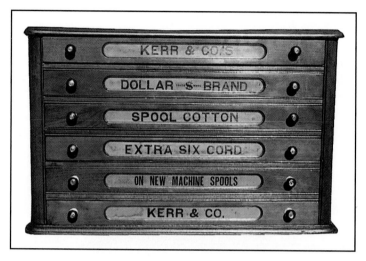

Kerr & Co.'s Dollar Brand Spool Cotton cabinet. $1,000 – 1,600.00. Courtesy of Harvey Leventhal

Whitlocks' Renowned Remedies cabinet with contents. Scarce. Both sides are tin embossed. $1,800.00 – 2,400.00. Courtesy of Harvey Leventhal.

Thread cabinet. Company not identified. $750.00 – 1,200.00.

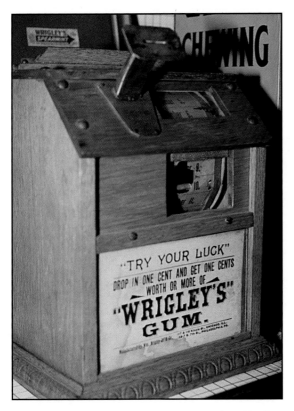

Wrigley's One-Cent Gum Dispenser. $1,600.00 – 2,500.00.

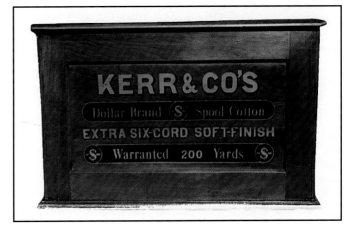

Kerr & Co.'s Dollar Brand Extra Six-Cord Soft Finish cabinet. $750.00 – 1,200.00.

Dr. A. C. Daniels Animal Medicines Cabinet. $2,200.00 – 3,400.00.

Belding's Silk cabinet. $1,000.00 – 1,500.00. Courtesy of Harvey Leventhal

1. *Milward's Helix Needles cabinet; 2. Clark's O.N.T. Spool cotton box; 3. Boyd Hook case. Advertising on the case states, "Better Than The Best Hook You Have Ever Used." Pat'd January 14, 1919 – December 16, 1919. 1. $425.00 – 600.00; 2. $85.00 – 135.00; 3. $215.00 – 275.00.* Courtesy of Harvey Leventhal

Eureka Silk & Twist cabinet with a clock. Elegant Victorian look. $1,400.00 – 2,200.00. Courtesy of Buffalo Bay Auction Co.

Lucky Strike advertising clock. R. A. Patterson Tobacco Companies. $2,500.00 – 3,500.00. Courtesy of Harvey Leventhal.

Interior store view showing several cabinets and showcases.

Humphrey's Specifics Remedy cabinet. $1,750.00 – 2,200.00.

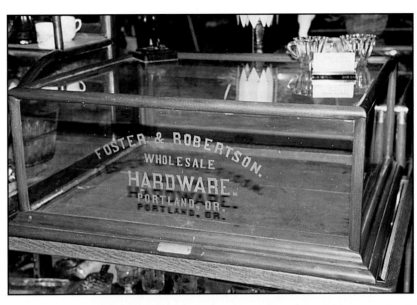

Foster & Robertson Wholesale Hardware oak-framed cabinet, Portland, Oregon. $375.00 – 600.00.

Postal unit. Oak construction. $1,750.00 – 2,600.00.

Lowney's Cocoa string holder. Two-sided. $2,200.00 – 2,750.00. Courtesy of Peter Crandall

Bike, coin gambling device. $2,000.00 – 3,400.00.

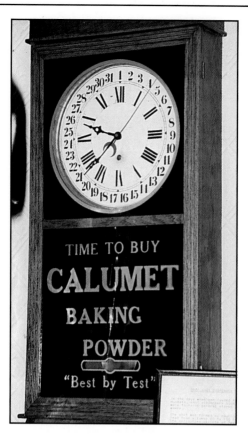

Calumet Baking Powder advertising clock. $1,750.00 – 3,000.00.

Regulator clock. This type of clock was frequently seen in general stores. $425.00 – 700.00.

Tea cabinet with four pull-out drawers. From a general store in West Virginia. $1,200.00 – 1,600.00. Wilson Collection

Scissors display case with revolving center section. J. B. F. Champlin & Son. $675.00 – 950.00. Wilson Collection

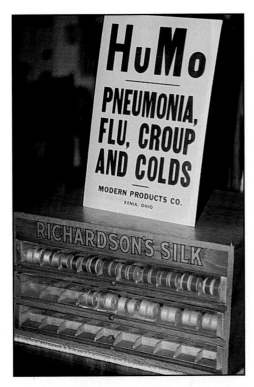

Three-drawer Richardson's Silk cabinet. $675.00 – 850.00. HuMo Pneumonia, Flu, Croup, and Colds counter sign, Xenia, Ohio. $50.00 – 75.00. Courtesy of Peter Crandall

Large display case with revolving center. $1,250.00 – 1,600.00. Courtesy of Peter Crandall

Checkerboard. Reverse painted on glass. Walnut frame with design. Checkerboards of all types, plain and fancy, were used by customers in general stores as a pleasant way to pass the time and catch up on the latest news. $225.00 – 400.00. Wilson Collection

A combination bag holder and string holder advertising John Hurd, Jobber in Wall Paper & Stationary (sic). Altoona, Pennsylvania. $525.00 – 750.00. *Courtesy of Peter Crandall*

Display sign from Day's Soap. The storekeeper could change the wording to please himself and, hopefully, generate some trade. $250.00 – 375.00. *Wilson Collection*

Store counter coffee grinder. Original condition. $1,275.00 – 1,800.00. *Courtesy of Peter Crandall*

U.S. Post Office General Delivery unit. $1,750.00 – 2,600.00.

KING OSCAR A GOOD CIGAR. Standing store broom holder. Sign is embossed. $675.00 – 950.00.

Chapter Three
⁖ TIN, WOODEN & OTHER CONTAINERS ⁖

In the very early days of the general store, most products came in bulk. The thought of individual containers for a variety of items was not given serious consideration.

There were few choices of brands. A customer would request some ground coffee, ginger, or perhaps some crackers. The storekeeper would then put the order together, weigh out what was necessary, and wrap each item. Paper bags were in the future. Mercantile stores received commodities in bulk from distant points. They were shipped overland or by water when possible. Barrels of flour and crackers, bags of cereals, fragrant coffee beans, and bulk wooden boxes of plug tobacco represented much of a store's inventory. Breakables were often shipped to merchants carefully placed in oatmeal.

Items such as nutmeg, pepper, and cloves were in peppercorn state and were ground at home on a grater or in a special grinder. Vinegar was pumped directly from the barrel, molasses was dispensed directly from the shipping hogshead, as were coal oil and other liquids. Tea was sold loose from a large counter canister at high prices. Dried peas, grains, beans, rice, and similar items were in large bins or built-in drawers.

Every sale was a custom order and every item was weighed out by the clerk, wrapped, tied with a string, and priced.

The era of bulk merchandising eventually raised some concern about sanitary conditions and accuracy of the scales and measurements.

The cracker barrel was a familiar container in early general stores. It was highly appreciated by store loungers who often took every opportunity to "dip in" for a free helping. The storekeeper was becoming increasingly concerned about "shrinkage" in the forms of pilfering, broken crackers, and staleness. The old cracker barrel days ended when the National Biscuit

Company packed its famous Uneeda Soda Crackers in a family-size moisture-proof pack in 1898.

By the turn of the century, multitudes of products came to the general store individually wrapped in tin containers, paper boxes, sealed bags, and bottles, carrying bright colored eye-appealing labels.

Name brands began to boom and their popularity was hastened by a variety of premiums that were offered to entice the customer. Frequent purchases of a particular product would be rewarded by a variety of gifts. Tempting new products were constantly showing up at the bustling crossroads stores. Tin and paper boxes were no longer made tediously by hand, but inexpensively by machine. The graphics on all the forms of packaging became very important. In spite of the promotion of such products, there was a strong core of prejudice against foods that couldn't be seen, sniffed, handled, and tasted, and there were many years of "we've never done it that way" to overcome. Early packaged goods were considered a curiosity long after their introduction.

In spite of the state of acceptance, goods continued to stream forward and found places on general store shelves everywhere. Bright red, green, yellow, and blue packages were decorated with eye-appealing trademarks and beautiful lithography.

The cereal industry found that packing was vital to survival. They soon found that packaging made their product much more appealing to a curious public and the sanitary benefits derived from packaging caused even wider acceptance.

The Pure Food and Drug Act of 1906 responded to the public's concern for sanitary products which hastened the packaging of a variety of goods.

The pace at the general store picked up. A tin of tobacco, a box of oatmeal, a can of wagon axle grease, a pail of coconut, or some cough drops from a glass dispenser were convenient to request at the store. Dr. Johnson's Educator Crackers; Newton's Heave, Cough, Distemper, and Indigestion Compound; Runkel Brothers Pure Breakfast Cocoa; Betsy Ross Shoe Polish; F. H. Leggett & Co.'s Standard Spices; Sunshine Krispy Crackers; Jumbo Peanut Butter; Adams Tutti Frutti Chewing Gum; Tiger White Rolled Oats; Heinz's India Relish; Grandpa's Wonder Soap; Moses Celebrated Cough Drops; and Honest Scrap Tobacco, to name a few, were available at number of mercantile stores throughout America.

Attractive colors and attention-getting paper labels with striking lithography created a loyal following and a strong demand for both established and new products. Tiger Chewing Tobacco, Snow Boy Washing Powder, Stickney & Poor's Spices, Jersey Cream Roasted Coffee, Baker's Cocoa, and Blanke's India Tea were all favorites of the day.

Merchants soon understood that packaging offered the benefits of less waste and more profits. Bulk products often spoiled. General stores were often home to a store cat. An open bag for oatmeal was a favorite resting place for the store cat, not to mention a frequent visiting place of mice at opportune times.

It was soon found that penny candy had a much longer life in air-tight glass containers and also permitted the customer to ponder his or her selections.

Major seed companies offered large wooden boxes with compartments to separate the various vegetable and flower seeds. The boxes could be immediately opened and placed in use. The interior covers and exterior panels were strong attention-getters with wonderful label illustrations.

It is clear that many early-day consumers considered the tin, wooden, paper, and glass containers much too beautiful and functional to discard. The beneficiary of this heritage is today's collector.

Front panel of Security Gas Colic Remedy. Remarkable horse illustrations. Price $1.00 per bottle. Certainly one of the finest vet remedy boxes. $95.00 – 155.00.
Courtesy of Ken Kennedy

Security Gas Colic Remedy. Rear panel. Security Remedy Co., Minneapolis, Minn. Uncle Sam illustration. Courtesy of Ken Kennedy

Mountain Herbaline Rose tin. Springsteen Medicine Co., Cleveland, Ohio. $12.00 – 20.00. Wilson Collection

Pan Work Confections Kiddy Kandies. California Peanut Co., Oakland, California. Tin pail. $275.00 – 425.00. Courtesy of Ken Kennedy

Rear portion of the Kiddy Kandies tin pail showing the delightful illustrations. Courtesy of Ken Kennedy

Left: Capital Poultry Food, Capital Stock Food Co., Helena, Montana. Right: International Distemper Remedy, International Stock Food Co., Minneapolis, Minn. Left, $65.00 – 95.00; right, $85.00 – 135.00. Courtesy of Ken Kennedy

Left to right: Clover Farm Coffee, $85.00 – 125.00; Ivanhoe Coffee, $115.00 – 175.00; Pilot-Knob Pure Coffee with bale handle, $225.00 – 400.00; Campbell Coffee with bale handle, $85.00 – 135.00; Union Club Coffee, $85.00 – 115.00. *Courtesy of Harvey Leventhal*

Milliken's Violet Talcum Powder. Celluloid. May be a sample dispenser. $350.00 – 525.00.
Courtesy of Harvey Leventhal

Dr. A. C. Daniels medicine bottles. Still have contents. $50.00 – 100.00 each. *Courtesy of Harvey Leventhal*

Dr. A. C. Daniels medicine containers. $35.00 – 65.00 each.
Courtesy of Harvey Leventhal

Dr. A. C. Daniels medicine containers. $35.00 – 65.00 each. *Courtesy of Harvey Leventhal*

Pilot-Knob Pure Coffee, bale handle. Bowers Brothers, Inc. $225.00 – 400.00. *Courtesy of Harvey Leventhal*

Ramon's Brownie Pills, counter glass jar. $235.00 – 425.00. *Wilson Collection*

Patent medicines. Left to right: Swamp Root, $21.00 – 28.00; Farr's Gray Hair Restorer, $32.00 – 45.00; Blackburn's MENTHO Laxene, $22.00 – 25.00; Radway's Ready Relief, $26.00 – 34.00. *Courtesy of Hook's Pharmacy, Indianapolis, Indiana*

Right: WALLA WALLA embossed chewing gum jar with American Indian. Left: Cabin jar. Right, $225.00 – 375.00; left, $275.00 – 425.00. Courtesy of Hooks Pharmacy, Indianapolis, Indiana

Planters Peanut embossed counter jar. $215.00 – 325.00. Courtesy of Hook's Pharmacy, Indianapolis, Indiana

Sanford's and Carter's ink bottles. $35.00 – 135.00. Courtesy of Hook's Pharmacy, Indianapolis, Indiana

Sanford's Ink bottles. $85.00 – 135.00. Courtesy of Hook's Pharmacy, Indianapolis, Indiana

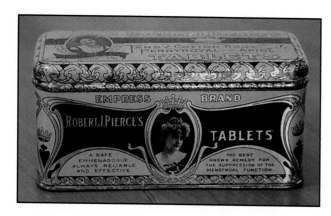

Robert J. Pierce's Tablets. Empress brand.
$45.00 – 58.00. Wilson Collection

Chichester's English Pennyroyal Pill containers and Beautyskin pocket mirror. Left to right: small tin, $35.00 – 65.00; "Chic" box, $42.00 – 65.00; large tin, $125.00 – 140.00; Chi-Ches-Ters pills, $30.00 – 45.00; tin on far right, $35.00 – 52.00; pocket mirror, $75.00 – 125.00. Courtesy of Harvey Leventhal

Large Hulman & Co.'s Combination Coffee container. $225.00 – 375.00. Courtesy of Hook's Pharmacy, Indianapolis, Indiana

Clark's O.N.T. spool thread box with illustration of two boys playing. $35.00 – 52.00. Courtesy of Harvey Leventhal

John Clark spool cotton box. $35.00 – 52.00. Courtesy of Harvey Leventhal

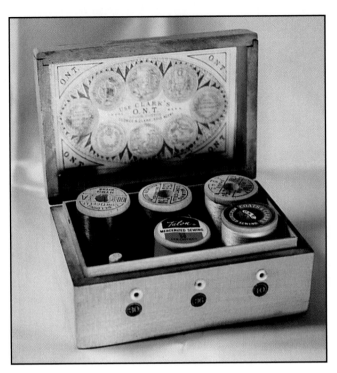

Clark's O.N.T. spool cotton box. $28.00 – 44.00. Courtesy of Harvey Leventhal

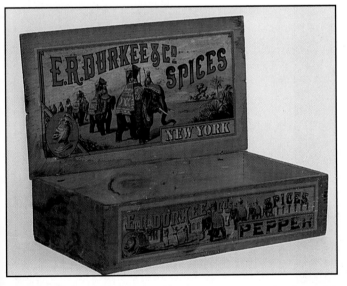

E. R. Durkee & Co. Spices, pepper. New York. Wooden box with colorful illustrations of elephants. $125.00 – 185.00. Courtesy of Ken Kennedy

Morning Glory Brand Ground Spices, mustard. Wooden box. $85.00 – 135.00. Courtesy of Ken Kennedy

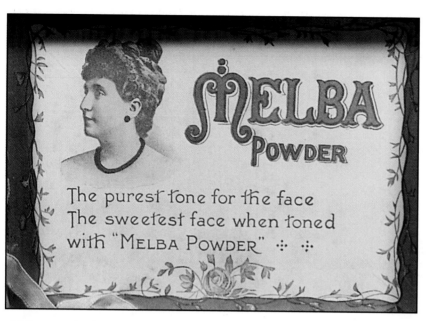

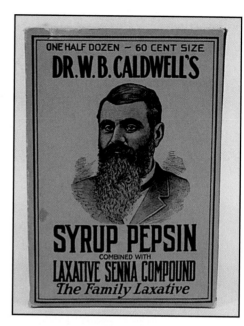

Melba Powder face powder. Small paper box. $22.00 – 35.00. Wilson Collection

Dr. W. B. Caldwell's Syrup Pepsin product box. $60.00 – 85.00. Wilson Collection

Patent medicines. $32.00 – 45.00. Courtesy of Hook's Pharmacy, Indianapolis, Indiana

Bust Developer Remedy. Interesting label. $40.00 – 48.00. Courtesy of Hook's Pharmacy, Indianapolis, Indiana

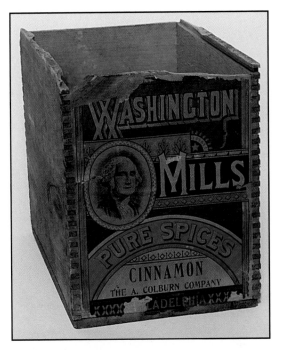

Washington Mills Pure Spices, cinnamon. Wooden box. $75.00 – 125.00. Courtesy of Ken Kennedy

Royal Liquid Bluing, glass bottle. Helwig & Leitch, Inc., Baltimore, Maryland. $50.00 – 75.00. Courtesy of Ken Kennedy

Indian Head Cream of Tartar. Wooden box. $125.00 – 185.00. Courtesy of Ken Kennedy

Security Gas Colic Remedy for Horses, Mules & Cattle. Security Remedy Co. $95.00 – 155.00. Courtesy of Ken Kennedy

Chas. Shaw & Son Spices. Wooden box. $75.00 – 125.00. Courtesy *of Ken Kennedy*

Blackman's Medicated Salt Brick display stand, $225.00 – 425.00; animal medicine boxes, $38.00 – 75.00. Courtesy of Ken Kennedy

Brook's Spool Cotton wooden box. $22.00 – 35.00. Courtesy of Harvey Leventhal

Mazawattee Tea. Illustration of Cinderella with her fairy godmother. Tin container. Beautiful illustrations on four sides. $475.00 – 625.00. Courtesy of Buffalo Bay Auction Co.

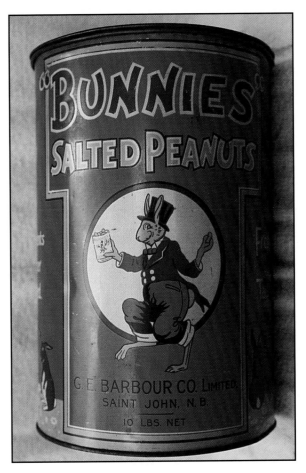

Spool box with wooden lid. $42.00 – 55.00. Courtesy of Harvey Leventhal

"Bunnies" Salted Peanuts. Large tin container. $300.00 – 425.00. Courtesy of Harvey Leventhal

Brook's Sewing Cottons, wooden box with an illustration of the factory. $95.00 – 125.00. Courtesy of Harvey Leventhal

Three small sewing thread boxes. $65.00 – 125.00. Courtesy of Harvey Leventhal

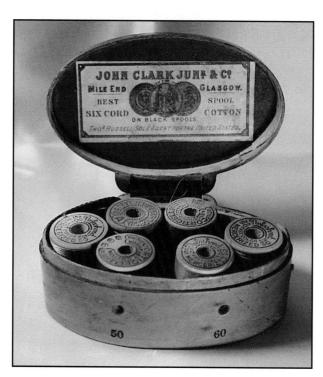

John Clark Spool Cotton wooden box. $75.00 – 110.00.
Courtesy of Harvey Leventhal

George A. Clark Spool Cotton wooden box.
$135.00 – 175.00. Courtesy of Harvey Leventhal

Clark's O.N.T. Spool Cotton box. $70.00 – 95.00.
Courtesy of Harvey Leventhal

Clark's O.N.T. Spool Cotton wooden box with illus-
tration of a cowboy inside the lid. $65.00 – 95.00.
Courtesy of Harvey Leventhal

Spool thread box with illustration of young girl on the lid. $75.00 – 105.00. Courtesy of Harvey Leventhal

Spool thread box with illustration of young girl on the inside lid. $45.00 – 70.00. Courtesy of Harvey Leventhal

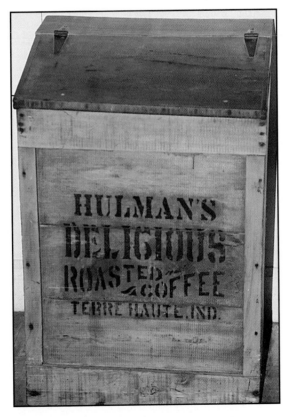

Hulman's Delicious Roasted Coffee wooden crate. Terre Haute, Ind. $215.00 – 275.00.

Huyler's Original Old-Fashioned Washington Taffy. $85.00 – 125.00. Wilson Collection

Mail Order House Teas & Coffees, Lanz Bros., Chicago, Illinois. $95.00 – 135.00.

Perfection Baking Powder. Stenciled tin container. $115.00 – 155.00.

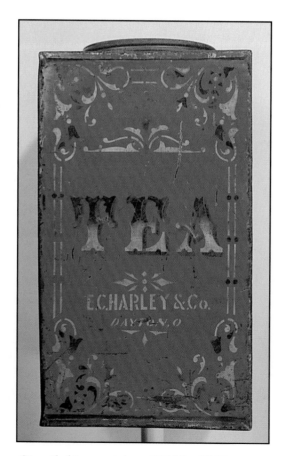

Stenciled tea container. $45.00 – 75.00.

Stenciled teas and coffees tin container. Chicago, Illinois. $85.00 – 135.00.

Towel's Syrup Bucket. Tin container. One-quart size. $155.00 – 210.00. *Courtesy of Buffalo Bay Auction Co.*

Minneapolis Breakfast Food cereal box. Circa 1910. International Food Co., Minneapolis, Minn. $135.00 – 250.00. *Courtesy of Buffalo Bay Auction Co.*

Jap Rose Soap wooden box. James S. Kirk & Co. $125.00 – 250.00. *Courtesy of en Kennedy*

Dilling's Jellies & Gum Drop tin container. Indianapolis, Indiana. $145.00 – 225.00. *Courtesy of Hook's Pharmacy, Indianapolis, Indiana*

Perfection Shredded Cocoanut, stenciled tin. $110.00 – 155.00.

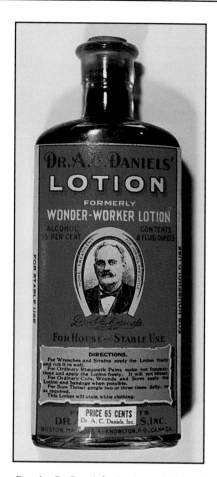

Dr. A. C. Daniels Lotion. Original bottle & contents. $50.00 – 100.00. Wilson Collection

Punch Polish mop. Round tin container. Chicago Mop & Polish Co., Chicago, Illinois. $85.00 – 125.00. Wilson Collection

Maryland Club Coffee bin. Baltimore, Maryland. $225.00 – 350.00.

Cataluna Penny Sticks Licorice. Wooden box with sliding top. $75.00 – 125.00. Wilson Collection

Silver Blend Brand Coffee. Davidson Grocery. Butte, Montana. $225.00 – 325.00. Courtesy of Buffalo Bay Auction Co.

Frontier 1846 Brand Pure Rolled Oats. Frontiersmen depicted on the front. Nave-McCord Mercantile Company, St. Joseph, Missouri. $200.00 – 275.00. Courtesy of Buffalo Bay Auction Co.

Convention Hall Coffee tin container. $250.00 – 375.00. Courtesy of Buffalo Bay Auction Co.

American Home Fresh Roasted Coffee. $175.00 – 265.00. Courtesy of Buffalo Bay Auction Co.

Left: Fairbanks Gold Dust Scouring Powder, $95.00 – 150.00; upper right: Fairbanks Gold Dust Scouring Powder; sample tin, $175.00 – 250.00; lower right: Fairbanks Gold Dust Scouring Cleanser, $110.00 – 175.00. *Courtesy of Buffalo Bay Auction Co.*

Atlas Kiln Dried Oats. Paper box. $135.00 – 225.00. *Courtesy of Buffalo Bay Auction Co.*

Hamill's Palm Brand Rolled Oats. S. Hamill Company, Keokuk, Iowa. $125.00 – 210.00. *Courtesy of Buffalo Bay Auction Co.*

Princess Rolled Oats. $95.00 – 175.00. *Courtesy of Buffalo Bay Auction Co.*

Robin Brand Rolled Oats. $95.00 – 175.00. *Courtesy of Buffalo Bay Auction Co.*

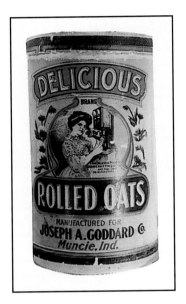

Robin Coffee. Paper label. $85.00 – 175.00. Courtesy of Buffalo Bay Auction Co.

Delicious Rolled Oats. Joseph A. Goddard Co., Muncie, Indiana. $110.00 – 215.00. Courtesy of Buffalo Bay Auction Co.

Knight's Sweet Pickles, barrel. $225.00 – 350.00. Courtesy of Peter Crandall

Washington Mills pepper. Wooden container. The A. Colburn Co., Philadelphia, Pennsylvania. $250.00 – 375.00. Courtesy of Peter Crandall

Red Cough Drops tin. Bone, Eagle & Co., Reading, Pa. $135.00 – 165.00. Courtesy of Peter Crandall

Boston Coffees Golden Rio store coffee container. Paper label. $325.00 – 525.00. Courtesy of Peter Crandall

The Franklin Biscuit Co. Steam Bakers, Philadelphia, Pennsylvania. Wooden with paper label. $135.00 – 185.00. Courtesy of Peter Crandall

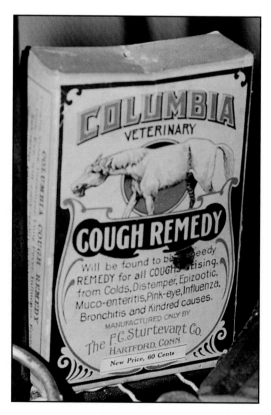

Saginaw Tips wooden matches. $145.00 – 175.00. Courtesy of Peter Crandall

Columbia Cough Remedy. F. C. Sturtevant Co., Hartford, Conn. $35.00 – 45.00. Wilson Collection

Bitters Remedies. Paper boxes. $22.00 – 30.00.

McLaughlin's Coffee sack, $14.00 – 22.00; Our Monogram Coffee, $37.00 – 48.00; White House Coffee, $32.00 – 40.00; Gold Bond Java Coffee sack, $26.00 – 35.00; Upper coffee container, $37.00 – 52.00; Lower coffee container, $35.00 – 45.00; Folger's Coffee sack, $12.00 – 20.00.

Liberty Brand Spices. Liberty Mills. Durand & Kasper Co., Chicago. $85.00 – 135.00.

H. J. Heinz Co., Pittsburgh, Pennsylvania. Store crock. $235.00 – 400.00. Courtesy of Buffalo Bay Auction Co.

Father Christmas holiday tin. $37.00 – 55.00. Wilson Collection

Deerwood Coffee. $175.00 – 300.00.
Courtesy of Buffalo Bay Auction Co.

Holiday Tea Tin. Two panel winter scenes.
$95.00 – 155.00. Wilson Collection

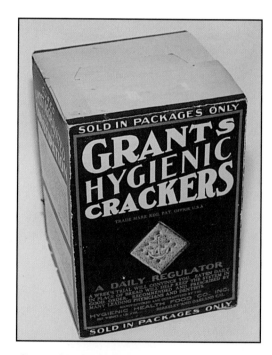

Grants Hygienic Crackers box. Paper. $27.00
– 42.00. Wilson Collection

Java & Mocha Knickerbocker Coffee. Chicago, Illinois. $65.00 – 95.00.

S. Hamill Company's Ke-O-Ka Blend Coffee. Keokuk, Iowa. $95.00 – 135.00.

Sweets Old Fashioned Stick Candy. Paper box. $24.00 – 38.00.

Overall detail of blacking box illustrated earlier in this chapter. $145.00 – 225.00. Wilson Collection

Farm Animal Louse Powder. Tin with handle. Battle, Hayward & Bower. $85.00 – 110.00. Wilson Collection

Close-up of previously illustrated tin to show the detail of the design. John H. Mann & Co. Wholesale & Retail Teas, Coffees & Spices. Syracuse, New York. $75.00 – 105.00. Wilson Collection

Merkel's Tooth Powder. Tin containers. Dayton, Ohio. $22.00 – 30.00 each. Wilson Collection

Slade's Allspice. Two paper containers with original contents. Boston, Mass. $17.00 – 25.00 each. Wilson Collection

Uncle Sam Oat Flakes. Biklen, Winzer Grocer Co., Burlington, Iowa. $95.00 – 210.00. Courtesy of Buffalo Bay Auction Co.

School Days Sifted Early Variety Peas. Paper label. $45.00 – 85.00. Courtesy of Buffalo Bay Auction Co.

Plymouth Rock Sweet Corn. Paper label. $45.00 – 85.00. Courtesy of Buffalo Bay Auction Co.

Chapter Four
❖ THE SPICE OF LIFE: BRANDS BY THE DOZEN ❖

Spices are aromatic flavorings made from parts of plants. They are native to tropical Asia and the Moluccas, or Spice Islands, of Indonesia. The early spice trade was a large enterprise and valued spices greatly. From the thirteenth century to the fifteenth century, Venice monopolized spice trade with the Middle East. Venice demanded such exorbitant prices, however, that Portugal and Spain looked eastward for routes to the Spice Islands around the Cape of Good Hope, and then, with the voyage of Christopher Columbus, searched westward. Although many of the early explorers were seeking gold, these expeditions gained much of their financial backing from trade in spices.

We are fortunate in today's world to have the easy availability of spices at reasonable prices. This occurred as a result of advances in commerce and shipping but also because many of the once-rare spices of the Orient have been naturalized in other parts of the world. In the early years of the old general store, spices were a relatively expensive commodity. Spices added a very welcome and pungent smell to the stores but, because of their origins and costs of importation, were considered an expensive specialty item.

Spices were originally dispensed in whole form to be ground or grated later by the customer. In the late nineteenth and early twentieth centuries, large tin containers were produced to provide storage for a variety of spices. They were usually attractively lithographed with striking designs featuring beautiful women, children, animals, and other subjects. In some cases, the name of the mercantile store was placed on the container. Often, however, the containers were not sold directly to the mercantile stores by the manufacturers or intermediaries, but were furnished to the distributors of the products involved who purchased them in quantity, painted and lettered to their specifications; the distributors in turn provided them to retail locations. Many mercantile stores boasted a complete set of colorful and elaborate containers dispensing allspice, mustard, cloves, cinnamon, cream of tartar, and ginger, among other spices.

Exotic styling representing distant and mystical lands was often used for a container's design. Some were lithographed, but many were elaborately painted. Some even included beveled plate-glass mirrors. I have a spice container in my collection that has a revolving metal wheel at the top. This made it easier for the proprietor to change the name as the contents changed. There were other containers that came with a slot and a variety of interchangeable names. The slot permitted the insertion and removal of the name of a particular spice as necessary.

The store customer would request a specific quantity of a particular spice and it would be removed from the appropriate large container and placed in a small paper packet.

After the turn of the century, transportation and distribution methods had become much more efficient which aided in lowering the cost of spices. At the same time, the packaging industry had also made great leaps. It was desirable to begin placing spices in small tin and paperboard containers. Once that change was made, products started flowing to the shelves of general stores. Local, regional, and national companies and distributors were eager to answer the demand. The style of packaging used in the early nineteenth century has survived to present times. Although the familiar style of container is still on the market, there has been a strong move to glass and plastic.

As this chapter illustrates, there appears to be an almost endless variety of brands with large numbers of containers surviving from the early 1900s through the 1940. There has been an escalated interest in very colorful and desirable spice containers in recent times. They have the benefits of availability and, due to their small size, demand little storage space. They are enthusiastically sought after and collected.

Many have survived in very good condition. I feel this is a function, to a large extent, of the contents. Spice products had a tendency to be placed in the pantry and used as needed. Frequently, the entire contents were never used but kept for that possible day when a particular recipe would require "a pinch of this" or "a dash of that."

Small spice containers can contain some remarkable graphics. For example, take a close look at the graphics of the following products: Farmers Pride Red Pepper, Pitkin's Old Home Paprika, Honey-Dew Allspice, Veteran Brand Nutmeg, Sunshine Cloves, White Villa Whole Cinnamon, and Honeymoon Brand Rubbed Sage.

The collecting possibilities are just as extensive as the multitudes of products that were made. There are paperboard and tin containers available. As would be expected in the wake of the collecting boom, the more scarce examples do not show up on the market as frequently. On the plus side, there were huge quantities of small spice containers produced. Exciting discoveries continue to await the collector.

Servu Pure Cassia. The McLean Co. Limited, Wholesale Grocers, Winnipeg, Manitoba. $225.00 – 350.00. Courtesy of Ken Kennedy

Hollywood Spices Mustard. Tin. Cupboard versions are priced lower. $250.00 – 400.00. Courtesy of Ken Kennedy

Jack Sprat Turmeric. Packed by Western Grocer Mills, Marshalltown, Iowa. $125.00 – 200.00. Courtesy of Ken Kennedy.

L-C-B Cinnamon. Lyle C. Brown Supply Co., Galesburg, Ill. $35.00 – 75.00. Courtesy of Ken Kennedy

Hills Bros. Highest Grade Sage. $55.00 – 125.00. Courtesy of Ken Kennedy

Max-I-Mum Allspice. $100.00 – 150.00. Courtesy of Ken Kennedy

McConnon's Pure Ground Spices/Ginger. $25.00 – 50.00. *Courtesy of Ken Kennedy.*

Ameta Pure Selected Thyme. The Independence Coffee & Spice Co., Denver, Colorado. $50.00 – 100.00. *Courtesy of Ken Kennedy*

Jack Sprat Turmeric. Western Grocer Mills, Marshalltown, Iowa. $35.00 – 60.00. *Courtesy of Ken Kennedy*

Liberty Cinnamon. Wetterau & Sons Grocer Co., St. Louis, Mo. $225.00 – 300.00. *Courtesy of Ken Kennedy*

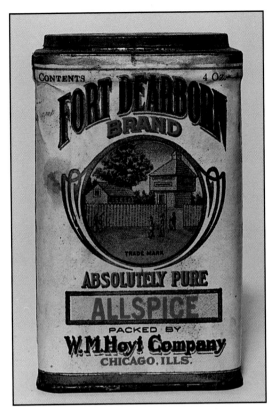

Monarch Brand Spices/Turmeric. Overwaitea Ltd., British Columbia. $75.00 – 135.00. Courtesy of Ken Kennedy

Fort Dearborn Allspice. W.M. Hoyt Company. Chicago, Illinois. $100.00 – 200.00. Courtesy of Ken Kennedy

Enterprise Turmeric. S. H. Tyler & Son, San Francisco, California. $75.00 – 125.00. Courtesy of Ken Kennedy

Meteor Spices/Turmeric. Lebanon Wholesale Grocer Co., Lebanon, Missouri. $75.00 – 125.00. Courtesy of Ken Kennedy

Par-A-Mount Pure Allspice. H. H. Cooper Ltd., Edmonton, Alberta. $175.00 – 250.00. Courtesy of Ken Kennedy

American Brand. The National Spice Co. Formerly D. R. James and Brother, New York. $110.00 – 215.00. Courtesy of Ken Kennedy

Hostess Cloves. Paul D. Newton & Co., Newark, New York. $110.00 – 215.00. Courtesy of Ken Kennedy

Amocat Cream Tartar. $75.00 – 135.00. Courtesy of Ken Kennedy

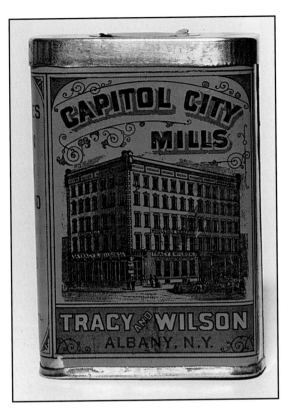

Capitol City Mills. Tracy and Wilson, Albany, New York. Early container. $200.00 – 325.00. *Courtesy of Ken Kennedy*

Nectar Turmeric. St. Louis Coffee & Spice Mills, St. Louis, Missouri. $40.00 – 65.00. *Courtesy of Ken Kennedy*

The Great Eastern Ground Spices/Cream Tartar. The Great Eastern Coffee & Tea Company. "The Leader Beats All." $75.00 – 165.00. *Courtesy of Ken Kennedy*

White Villa Pure Spices/Allspice. White Villa Grocers, Inc., Cincinnati-Dayton, Ohio. $60.00 – 95.00. *Courtesy of Ken Kennedy*

Home Brand Turmeric. Griggs, Cooper & Co., St. Paul, Minn.; Austin, Minn.; Fargo, N.D.; Minot, N.D.; Aberdeen, S.D. $22.00 – 40.00. Courtesy of Ken Kennedy

National Ground Spices/Cream Tartar. Geo. Rasmussen Co., Chicago; Minneapolis; Milwaukee; Des Moines. $35.00 – 60.00. Courtesy of Ken Kennedy

Burma Spices/Turmeric. Empire Spice Mills. Chicago, Ill. $22.00 – 42.00. Courtesy of Ken Kennedy

Roundup Spices/Turmeric. Roundup Grocery Co. $235.00 – 365.00. Courtesy of Ken Kennedy

Index Pure Spices/Allspice. Elliott Grocery Co., Logansport, Indiana. $70.00 – 125.00. Courtesy of Ken Kennedy

Wedding Breakfast Whole Black Pepper. Nash-Smith T. & C. Co., St. Louis and Denver. $60.00 – 130.00. Courtesy of Ken Kennedy

Imperial Mustard. Gray Manufacturing Co., Spokane, Washington. $185.00 – 275.00. Courtesy of Ken Kennedy

Frontier 1846 Brand Red Pepper. Nave McCord Mercantile Co., St. Joseph, Missouri. $225.00 – 340.00. Courtesy of Ken Kennedy

Honeymoon Pure Spices/Red Pepper. O. J. Moore Grocer Co., Sioux City, Iowa. $175.00 – 240.00. Courtesy of Ken Kennedy

Ben-Hur Pure Jamaica Ginger. $20.00 – 40.00. Courtesy of Ken Kennedy

Ben-Hur Pure Mustard. $20.00 – 40.00. Courtesy of Ken Kennedy

Roundup Mace. Roundup Grocery Co. $125.00 – 240.00. Courtesy of Ken Kennedy

Snow-Ball Pure Spices/Cinnamon. $115.00 – 200.00.
Courtesy of Ken Kennedy

Oak Hill Turmeric. E. C. Hall Company, Brockton, Mass. $125.00 – 170.00. Courtesy of Ken Kennedy

Wixon Allspice. Wixon Spice Co., Chicago, Ill. $65.00 – 130.00. Courtesy of Ken Kennedy

Lake View Whole Cinnamon. Mallott-Johnson Co., Chicago, Illinois. $175.00 – 300.00. Courtesy of Ken Kennedy

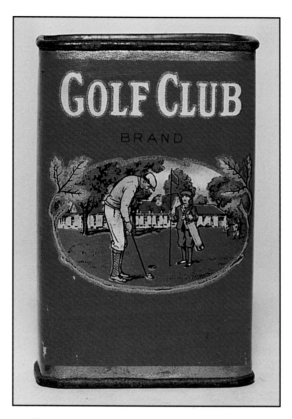

Puck Ground Allspice. "Worth The Money." Puck Food Products, New York; Memphis. $105.00 – 185.00. Courtesy of Ken Kennedy

Golf Club Brand Spices. $175.00 – 325.00. Courtesy of Ken Kennedy

Dove Brand Mustard. The Frank Tea & Spice Co., Cincinnati, Ohio. $55.00 – 105.00. Courtesy of Ken Kennedy

Busy Biddy Cream Tartar. $145.00 – 265.00. Courtesy of Ken Kennedy

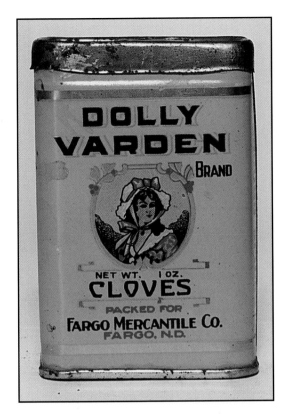

Dolly Varden Cloves. Fargo Mercantile Co., Fargo, N. D. $110.00 – 200.00. Courtesy of Ken Kennedy

Old Judge Spices/Allspice. David G. Evans Coffee Co., St. Louis, Mo. $22.00 – 44.00. Courtesy of Ken Kennedy

Genuine Three Crow White Pepper. The Atlantic Spice Co., Rockland, Maine. $35.00 – 75.00. Courtesy of Ken Kennedy

Mohican Pure Spices/Mace. $120.00 – 185.00. Courtesy of Ken Kennedy

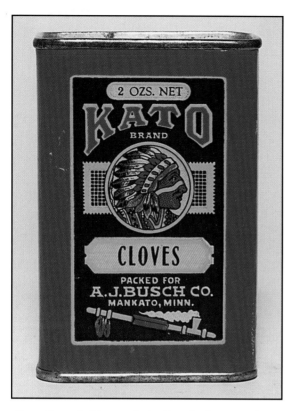

Kato Brand Cloves. A. J. Busch Co., Mankato, Minn. $75.00 – 155.00. Courtesy of Ken Kennedy

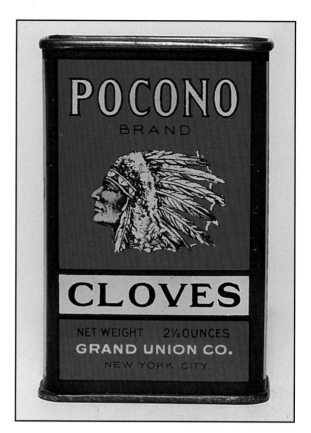

Pocono Brand Cloves. Grand Union Co., New York City. $165.00 – 250.00. Courtesy of Ken Kennedy

Blackbird Pure Ground Brand Turmeric. $60.00 – 95.00.
Courtesy of Ken Kennedy

Bell's Poultry Seasoning. $70.00 – 115.00. Courtesy of Ken Kennedy

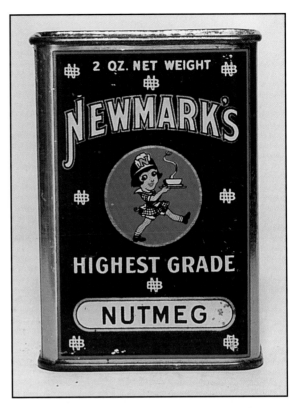

Busy Biddy Pure Spices/Allspice. Davis-Strauss-Stauffer Co., Allentown; Bangor; Easton; Stroudsburg, Pa. $95.00 – 115.00. Courtesy of Ken Kennedy

Newmark's Highest Grade Nutmeg. $115.00 – 175.00. Courtesy of Ken Kennedy

Juno Brand Ginger. The McClintock-Trunkey Co., Spokane, Washington. $55.00 – 120.00. Courtesy of Ken Kennedy

Buster Brown Cinnamon. Jas. H. Forbes Tea & Coffee Co., St. Louis, Mo. $120.00 – 175.00. Courtesy of Ken Kennedy

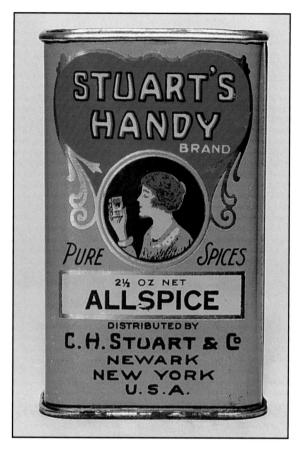

Stuart's Handy Allspice. C. H. Stuart & Co., Newark;
New York. $55.00 – 115.00. Courtesy of Ken Kennedy

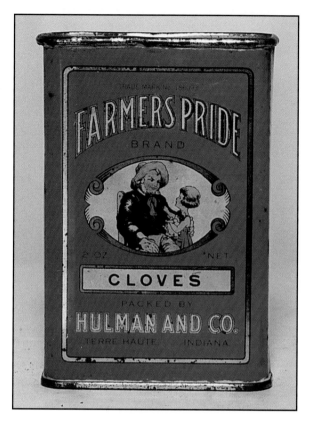

Farmers Pride Cloves. Hulman & Co., Terre Haute,
Indiana. Tin container. $95.00 – 165.00. Courtesy of
Ken Kennedy

Fairway Curry Powder. $65.00 – 125.00. Courtesy
of Ken Kennedy

Empress Parsley. Empress Mfg. Co., Ltd., Vancouver,
B. C. $60.00 – 112.00. Courtesy of Ken Kennedy

Anchor Cinnamon. David G. Evans Coffee Co., St. Louis, Mo. $25.00 – 60.00. *Courtesy of Ken Kennedy*

Chef Allspice. The Berdan Co., Toledo, Ohio. $75.00 – 135.00. *Courtesy of Ken Kennedy*

Sunbonnet Spices Cream Tartar. Indianapolis Fancy Grocery Co., Indianapolis, Indiana. $110.00 – 175.00. *Courtesy of Ken Kennedy*

Mother's Joy Allspice. "Always Satisfies." $120.00 – 215.00. *Courtesy of Ken Kennedy*

Columbia Cloves. Sutherland & McMillan, Pittston, Pa. $210.00 – 300.00. Courtesy of Ken Kennedy

Dove Brand Rubbed Sage. $95.00 – 155.00. Courtesy of Ken Kennedy

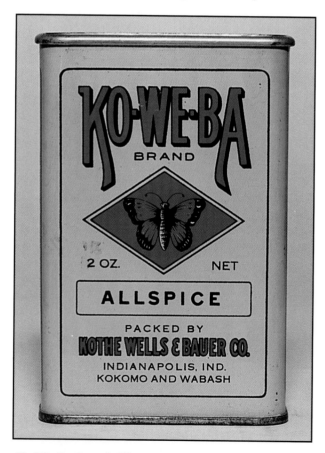

Ko-We-Ba Brand Allspice. Kothe Wells & Bauer Co., Indianapolis, Ind.; Kokomo and Wabash. $120.00 – 175.00. Courtesy of Ken Kennedy

Grisdale Ground Sage. Gristede Bros., Inc., New York. $55.00 – 125.00. Courtesy of Ken Kennedy

Faust Ginger. C. F. Blanke Tea & Coffee Co., St. Louis.
$55.00 – 125.00. Courtesy of Ken Kennedy

Folger's Golden Gate Allspice. $55.00 – 110.00.
Courtesy of Ken Kennedy

Iris Brand Allspice. $115.00 – 175.00.
Courtesy of Ken Kennedy

Group photo of spice tins that are illustrated in this chapter. Very interesting designs generally on small containers.
Courtesy of Ken Kennedy

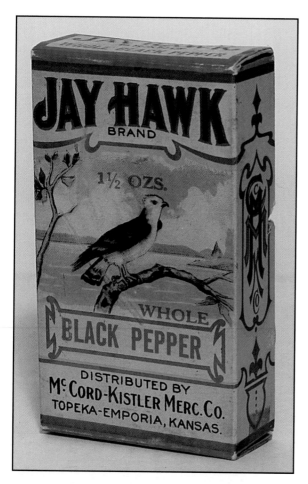

Jay Hawk Whole Black Pepper. McCord-Kistler Mercantile Co., Topeka-Emporia, Kansas. $35.00 – 70.00. Courtesy of Ken Kennedy

Regoes Rubbed Sage. Rigo Manufacturing Company, Nashville, Tenn. $55.00 – 95.00. Courtesy of Ken Kennedy

Honeymoon Brand Rubbed Sage. $95.00 – 165.00. Courtesy of Ken Kennedy

WGY Ground Cloves. W. G. Y. Food Products Co., Inc., Schenectady, New York. $105.00 – 145.00. Courtesy of Ken Kennedy

Pitkin's Old Home Pure Spices/Cloves. J. M. Pitkin & Co. $65.00 – 115.00. Courtesy of Ken Kennedy

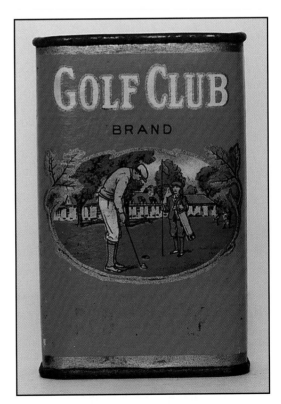

Golf Club Brand Spices. Another variation. $175.00 – 325.00. Courtesy of Ken Kennedy

Moshier Brothers Gilt Edge Spices, Utica, New York. Large store tin. $325.00 – 750.00. *Courtesy of Ken Kennedy*

Grossmans Pure Arena Ground Spices. William Grossman Co., Milwaukee, Wis. Early stenciled store tin. $145.00 – 175.00.

Imperial Brand Mustard. Gray Manufacturing Co., Spokane, Washington. Another example previously illustrated. $215.00 – 325.00. *Courtesy of Ken Kennedy*

Amocat Brand Mace. $75.00 – 135.00. *Courtesy of Ken Kennedy*

Pure Ground Spices/Mustard. Durand-McNeil-Horner Co., Chicago, Illinois. Large stenciled store tin container. $185.00 – 275.00.

Hatch & Jenks Pure Ground Cinnamon. Buffalo, New York. Large stenciled store tin container. $135.00 – 250.00. Wilson Collection

Shores Selected Spices/Allspice. Shores Farm Remedy Co., Tripoli, Iowa. $85.00 – 145.00. Courtesy of Ken Kennedy

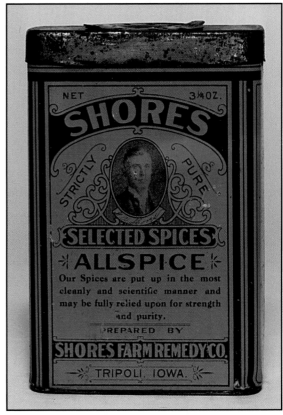

Left to right: Royal Spice Mills Black Pepper, The Clawson Company, Philadelphia, wooden box, $75.00 – 125.00; Cream Tartar store bin, $140.00 – 225.00; Ginger store bin, $175.00 – 300.00. Courtesy of Peter Crandall

Ward Spices/Ground Sage. George B. Almy, Inc., Albany, New York. $125.00 – 175.00. Courtesy of Ken Kennedy

Wm. Edwards & Co. Mustard. Large tin store container. The mustard display area rotates to other spices to indicate the actual contents. Cleveland, Ohio. $375.00 – 675.00. Wilson Collection

Advertising sign for Forest City Baking Powder. Vouwie Brothers, Cleveland, Ohio. $44.00 –75.00. Wilson Collection

Arena Spices/Allspice. Wm. Grossman Co. Milwaukee, Wis. $55.00 – 95.00

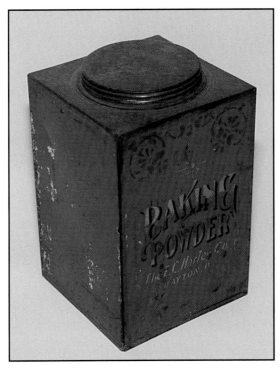

Baking powder stenciled store tin container. The F. C. Harley Co., Dayton, Ohio. $38.00 – 75.00. Wilson Collection

Acropolis Brand Pure Ground White Pepper. $95.00 – 155.00. Courtesy of Ken Kennedy

An incredible collection of spice containers. The variety of brands and the conditions of the containers are amazing. Courtesy of Ken Kennedy

Chapter Five
✦ EARLY STORE ADVERTISING ✦

Collecting early advertising posters, broadsides, counter displays, hanging trade signs, or anything else used in promoting the sale of merchandise has captured the interest of a large number of collectors. As a result, superior advertising items have experienced a significant escalation in price over the past dozen years.

Paper signs are now demanding prices that were previously reserved for those produced in tin. Some collectors consider high-end advertising signs to merit the category of an art form, and I agree. Many of the signs produced in the late nineteenth and early twentieth centuries are incredible examples of early artists working at top form.

America was on the move during the glory years of the old general store. New companies were evolving and anxious to generate an identity. Advertising in the form of posters, tin signs, and broadsides was considered an expedient manner in which to gain customers.

Familiar names such as Pillsbury Flour, Lipton Tea, Luden's Cough Drops, Hills Brothers Coffee, Campbell Soups, and Burpee Seeds were growing companies and have survived to modern times. Many others lasted a short period and simply disappeared from history.

It was hardly possible to enter an early general store without observing a variety of advertising signs. Everything from Ferry's Seeds to Winchester ammunition may have occupied a prominent position on the wall. Drummers and tradesmen were always anxious to leave behind a reminder of the products they promoted. Exterior walls were frequently plastered with auction broadsides, patent medicine ads, tobacco posters, and anything else that could be tacked up with the approval of the storekeeper. Harsh weather conditions destroyed these exterior signs within a period of time, but fresh ones always seemed to appear to replace those that were damaged.

It was inside the store that signs survived the passing of months and years. Many were tacked up above the shelves and left in their original position for years. Chase and Sanborn's products and Arbuckle's Coffee were heavily advertised and their signs found favor with general store owners.

Storekeepers were generally eager to accept free advertising signs and often proud to display them. I once visited an old general store in a rural area of Kansas that still had advertising signs from the early 1900s proudly hanging in the store. Much to my disappointment, the owner was not willing to sell those that were displayed but mentioned he had a "few" in the basement that might interest me. That was the understatement of the year. I eagerly followed him to the basement of the store and was directed to a storage area. Some of the most incredible signs I have ever seen were stacked up. But as I began to examine them closely in dim lighting, extreme displeasure set in. Over the years, moisture and mildew had ruined them to the point that they were not salvageable.

As I view collections of early advertising signs, I am always amazed at the incredible numbers and types that were produced. Not a week or two goes by that I do not see a sign or store advertising item that I have not seen previously. I have been fortunate to add some of them to my collection. As all collectors do, I sometimes dwell on those that "got away."

I feel that the type of advertising signs illustrated in this chapter provide a window to the past and an appreciation of a time in America that is long gone. More importantly, though, the era still lives in the hearts of collectors everywhere.

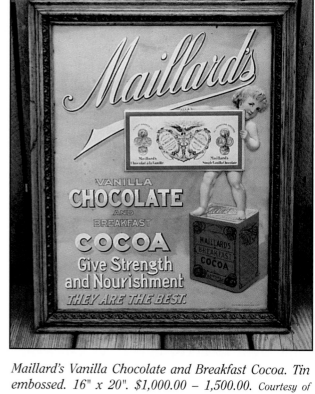

Maillard's Vanilla Chocolate and Breakfast Cocoa. Tin embossed. 16" x 20". $1,000.00 – 1,500.00. Courtesy of Harvey Leventhal

Hy-Quality Coffee. Girl in swing. $500.00 – 800.00. Courtesy of Harvey Leventhal

Standard Solid Leather Star Brand Shoes. Paper. $150.00 – 250.00. Courtesy of Harvey Leventhal

Kellogg's Corn Flakes. Framed die-cut stand-up. $175.00 – 250.00. Courtesy of Harvey Leventhal

Willimantic Spool Cotton sign. Paperboard. 27" x 34".
$250.00 – 400.00. Courtesy of Harvey Leventhal

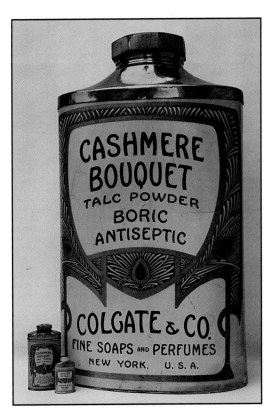

Cashmere Bouquet Talc Powder. Counter display. $950.00 – 1,250.00. Courtesy of Harvey Leventhal

Pabst Malt Extract. Die-cut ad. $9.00 – 15.00.

Buckingham's Dye for the Whiskers. R. P. Hall & Co. Nashua, New Hampshire. Paper. Die-cut. $725.00 – 1,050.00

New Home Sewing Machine Company. Paper.
$475.00 – 725.00.

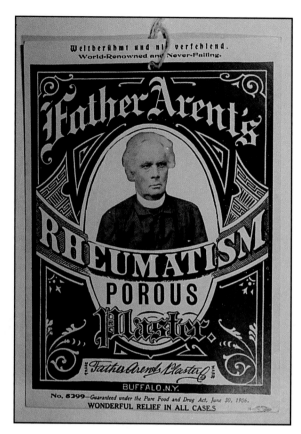

Father Arent's Rheumatism Porous Plaster.
Buffalo, New York. Heavy paper hanging ad.
$32.00 – 45.00. Wilson Collection

Elastic Starch. Die-cut. Heavy paper. $245.00 – 350.00.

Hostetter's Celebrated Stomach Bitters. Paper. $325.00 – 450.00.

Valet Auto Strop Razor. Heavy paper. $275.00 – 350.00.

Father John's Medicine. Heavy paper. $155.00 – 250.00. Wilson Collection

Adams Pepsin Tutti-Frutti Gum. $425.00 – 675.00.

Helmar Turkish Cigarettes. Reverse wall-mounted. Porcelain flange die-cut. $575.00 – 800.00.

Liberty Lanterns. Die-cut paperboard ad. $425.00 – 650.00. Courtesy of the Vermont Country Store

Johnson Halter. Horse head advertising the product. $525.00 – 750.00. Courtesy of Warp's Pioneer Village

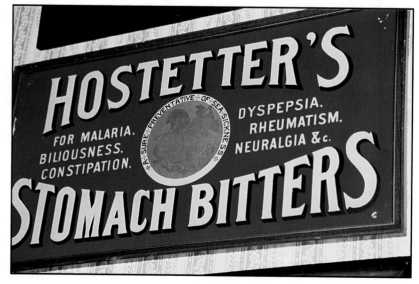

Murine Eye Tonic. Paperboard. $650.00 – 825.00. Courtesy of Hook's Pharmacy

Hostetter's Stomach Bitters. Tin. $1,250.00 – 1,600.00.

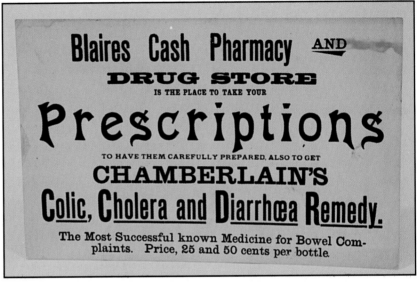

Borax paperboard die-cut sign. "Borax Bill Jr." $450.00 – 750.00. Wilson Collection

Blaires Cash Pharmacy Drug Store. Prescriptions. Chamberlain's Colic, Cholera, and Diarrhea Remedy. Heavy paper. $22.00 – 32.00. Wilson Collection

Watches Jewelry Clocks trade sign. Wood. $925.00 – 1,450.00.

Ivory Soap. Paper. Original frame. Paper. $1,750.00 – 2,400.00. Courtesy of Hook's Pharmacy

Arm & Hammer Soda. A perplexed hunter. Paperboard. $325.00 – 475.00. *Courtesy of Vermont Country Store*

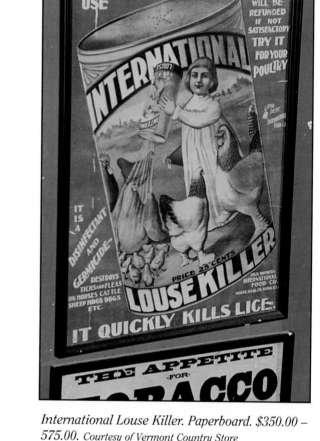

International Louse Killer. Paperboard. $350.00 – 575.00. *Courtesy of Vermont Country Store*

Columbia Vet Remedies. Statue of horse. Plaster of Paris. $525.00 – 750.00.

Brown's Jumbo Bread. Tin litho die-cut. 15" x 13". Circa 1910. $375.00 – 550.00. *Courtesy of Buffalo Bay Auction Co.*

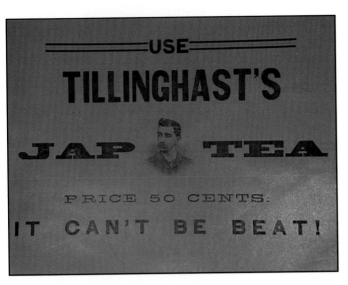

Tillinghast's Jap Tea. Heavy paper. $25.00 – 40.00. Wilson Collection

Lambertville "Snag-Proof" Rubber Boots & Shoes. Tin. 15" x 19". $800.00 – 1,200.00. Courtesy of Harvey Leventhal

J. & P. Coats Spool Cotton. Pressed fiber-board. 18" x 30". $500.00 – $1,000.00. Courtesy of Harvey Leventhal

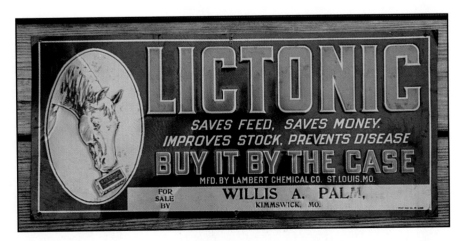

Lictonic Stock Remedy. Embossed tin. 19½" x 8½". $250.00 – 450.00. Courtesy of Harvey Leventhal

J. & P. Coats Spool Cotton. 18" x 24". Paper. Dated 1872. $300.00 – 500.00. Courtesy of Harvey Leventhal

Mennen's Toilet Powder. Large store display. Paper on cardboard. $1,850.00 – 2,750.00. Courtesy of Harvey Leventhal

Oak-Leaf Soap. Gowans & Stover. Buffalo, New York. Paper. Dated 1889. 12" x 31". $1,000.00 – 1,500.00. Courtesy of Harvey Leventhal

Dr. Haile's "Ole Injun" System Tonic. Large paperboard sign. $225.00 – 350.00. Courtesy of Peter Crandall

Fletcher's Castoria. Large paperboard sign. $275.00 – 500.00. Courtesy of Peter Crandall

Havana Ribbon 5 Cent Cigar. Die-cut paperboard counter display. $275.00 – 450.00. Courtesy of Peter Crandall

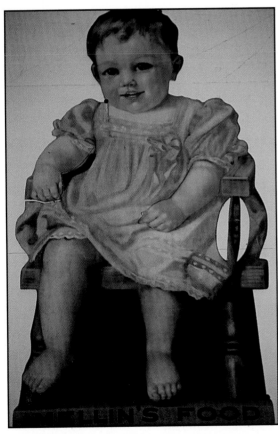

Mellin's Food. Die-cut paperboard counter display. $325.00 – 575.00. Courtesy of Peter Crandall

W.L. Douglas Shoes. Self-framed tin sign. $1,250.00 – 1,900.00. Courtesy of Peter Crandall

Aunt Jemima Pancake Flour. Aunt Jemima in swing. $3,200.00 – 5,500.00. *Courtesy of Peter Crandall*

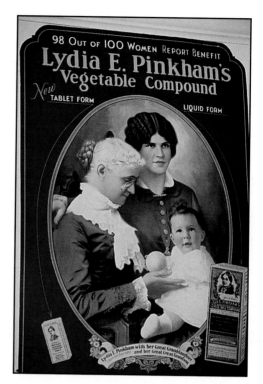

Lydia E. Pinkham's Vegetable Compound. Large paperboard poster. $1,650.00 – 2,750.00. *Courtesy of Peter Crandall*

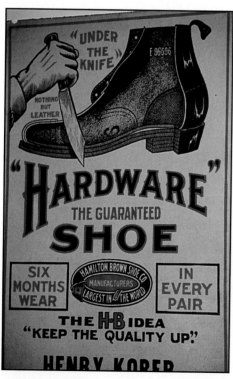

Hardware Shoe. Heavy paper sign. $135.00 – 225.00. *Courtesy of Peter Crandall*

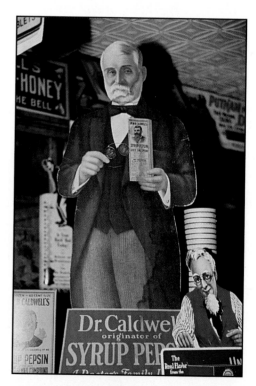

Dr. Caldwell's Syrup Pepsin. Large standing paperboard die-cut sign. $650.00 – 825.00. *Courtesy of Peter Crandall*

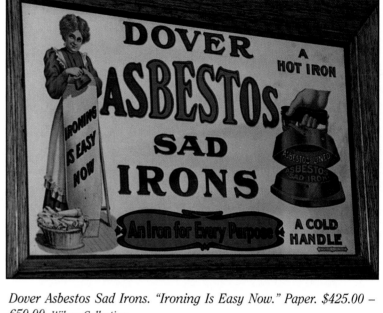

Dr. Caldwell's Syrup Pepsin. Large paperboard sign. $650.00 – 825.00. Courtesy of Peter Crandall

Dover Asbestos Sad Irons. "Ironing Is Easy Now." Paper. $425.00 – 650.00. Wilson Collection

J. F. Millemann & Co. Eagle Brand Ham. New York. Paperboard. $400.00 – 625.00.
Wilson Collection

Pheasant Brand Pure Lard. The Cincinnati Abattoir Co., Cincinnati, Ohio. U.S. inspected and passed under the act of Congress of June 30, 1906. $225.00 – 375.00.
Wilson Collection

F. S. Hurlbut & Co. Millinery and Straw Goods. Cleveland, Ohio. Spring and Summer 1887. Paper. $375.00 – 500.00. Wilson Collection

Burson Clothing Co. Carey, Ohio. Christmas ad with Old St. Nick. $225.00 – 350.00. Wilson Collection

Magic Yeast. For Making Bread • For Making Root Beer • For Making Buckwheat Cakes. Paper. $300.00 – 400.00. Courtesy of Buffalo Bay Auction Co.

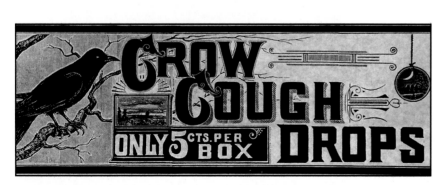

Crow Cough Drops, Only 5 Cents Per Box. $135.00 – 185.00. Wilson Collection

Campbell's Horse Foot Remedy. The James B. Campbell Co., Chicago. Paper. $475.00 – 700.00. *Courtesy of Warp's Pioneer Village*

Camay Toilet Soap. Tin litho. 27" x 6". 1915. $375.00 – 550.00. *Courtesy of Buffalo Bay Auction Co.*

Postum Food Coffee. If Coffee don't agree, use Postum Food Coffee. Heavy paperboard. $525.00 – 750.00. *Wilson Collection*

Gold Medal Camp Furniture. Gold Medal Camp Furniture Mfg. Co., Racine, Wis. Self-framed tin lithograph. $900.00 – 1,200.00. *Courtesy of Buffalo Bay Auction Co.*

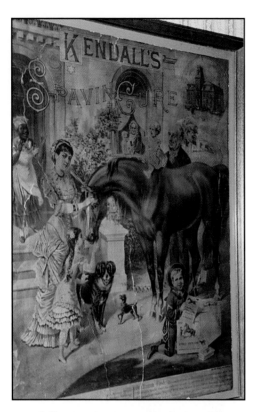

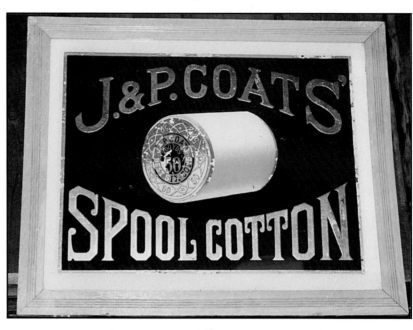

Kendall's Spavin Cure. $375.00 – 650.00.
Paper. Courtesy of Hook's Pharmacy

J. & P. Coats' Spool Cotton. Pressed fiberboard. 18" x 30". $525.00 – 950.00.
Courtesy of Harvey Leventhal

Copco Bath Soap. The N. K. Fairbank Co.
Paper. $375.00 – 450.00.

Carter's Ink. $1,275.00 – 2,600.00.

Lavine Soap & Washing Powder. Paper. Hartford Chemical Co., Hartford, Conn. $500.00 – 700.00. Courtesy of Buffalo Bay Auction Co.

Post Toasties. Paper. $175.00 – 300.00. Courtesy of Buffalo Bay Auction Co.

Deering Harvesting Machines. 1907 calendar. $150.00 – 225.00. Courtesy of Buffalo Bay Auction Co.

Professor Horsford's Baking Powder. $375.00 – 650.00. Courtesy of Buffalo Bay Auction Co.

Levi Strauss & Co. Paper. $525.00 – 850.00. Courtesy of Buffalo Bay Auction Co.

The Fair. Dry Goods, Millinery, Furs & Groceries. 1908 calendar. $175.00 – 250.00. Courtesy of Buffalo Bay Auction Co.

The Snyder Mercantile Co., Washtucna, Washington. Calendar. Advertisement for Selz Shoes. $450.00 – 750.00. Courtesy of Buffalo Bay Auction Co.

Foot Rest Hosiery. Paper. $375.00 – 650.00. Courtesy of Buffalo Bay Auction Co.

Fleischmann's Yeast. Paper.
$250.00 – 400.00. Courtesy of
Buffalo Bay Auction Co.

Pears' Soap. Paper. $350.00 – 475.00.
Courtesy of Buffalo Bay Auction Co.

Purity Fruit. P. Brucato & Co., New York.
$525.00 – 700.00. Courtesy of Buffalo Bay Auction
Co.

Deere Vehicles. "Deere Vehicles Are All Right." $625.00 – 850.00.
Courtesy of Buffalo Bay Auction Co.

Mother's Oats. Akron, Ohio. Advising customers that this 17" x 24" illustration (without advertising) can be requested with cut-outs from two packages of the product along with 4 cents in stamps (Boy No. 4). $325.00 – 550.00. Courtesy of Buffalo Bay Auction Co.

Mother's Oats. Akron, Ohio. Same as at left but illustrating Boy No. 3. $325.00 – 550.00. Courtesy of Buffalo Bay Auction Co.

Independent Tea Co. Teas, Coffees & Baking Powder. Kalamazoo, Michigan. Die-cut calendar. 1909. $325.00 – 450.00. Courtesy of Buffalo Bay Auction Co.

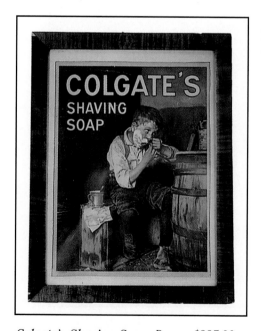

Colgate's Shaving Soap. Paper. $285.00 – 350.00. Courtesy of Buffalo Bay Auction Co.

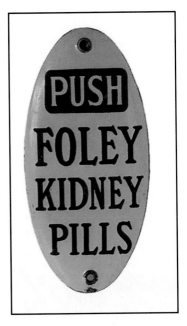

Foley Kidney Pills. Tin door push. $225.00 – 300.00.
Courtesy of Buffalo Bay Auction Co.

Singer Sewing Machines. Advertising calendar. 1892. $175.00 – 250.00. Courtesy of Buffalo Bay Auction Co.

Howe Scale. Trade card. There appears to be a serious "honest weight" problem going on. $4.00 – 8.00. Wilson Collection

Hills Bros. Coffee. Embossed tin. Circa 1910. $400.00 – 600.00. Courtesy of Buffalo Bay Auction Co.

Satin Powder & Satin Skin Cream. Paper. Large poster. 1903. Albert F. Wood, M'F'R. The Satin Toilet Specialties. Detroit, Mich. $275.00 – 425.00.
Wilson Collection

Superior. The Superior Drill Co., Springfield, Ohio. $450.00 – 650.00. Wilson Collection

S. B. Kitchel's Liniment. Paper broadside. Kitchel's Liniment — A Friend of Horse and Owner. $22.00 – 35.00. Wilson Collection

*Campfire Marshmallows. Heavy cardboard. Circa 1912. $525.00 –
750.00. Courtesy of Buffalo Bay Auction Co.*

*Swift's Premium Ham. Original frame. Swift & Co. $650.00 – 825.00.
Courtesy of Buffalo Bay Auction Co.*

*Vander Bie's Ice Cream. Die-cut Father Christmas. $375.00 – 450.00.
Courtesy of Buffalo Bay Auction Co.*

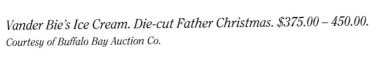

Union Made men's hat tin sign. The United Hatters of North America. $750.00 – 900.00. Courtesy of Buffalo Bay Auction Co.

Genuine Butter-Nut Bread advertising sign. $375.00 – 650.00.
Courtesy of Buffalo Bay Auction Co.

Murray & Lanman's Florida Water Perfume. Trade card.
$5.00 – 8.00. Courtesy of Ann Heuer

Chapter Six
⊱ THE TOBACCO COUNTER ⊰

It was an era when most adult males used tobacco products. To meet the demand, the general store dedicated significant space to a variety of tobacco products. Cut plug, "seegars," pipes, snuff, and other items were readily available and often competed for room on the crowded shelves and in cases. Many crossroads community and small towns did not have specialty tobacco stores. This caused a regular customer to make frequent trips to the general store's tobacco counter and request his favorite brand.

The brand names were endless. Old Slug, My Sweetheart, Scalping Knife, Richmond Belle, Pike's Peak, Gold Brick, Rock Bottom, Sitting Bull, Black Bass, Legal Tender, Hard Pan, and It's Naughty, But Oh How Nice were just a small number available. Brand loyalty developed and, to some extent, specific brands became good sellers in certain locations. By 1870 naming plug tobacco became a challenging and interesting pastime. Trends of the day were always considered. Free Silver and Union Boy reflected the labor events of the day, and names like Day's Work and Farmer's Pride were favorites of rural folk.

Tobacco products were offered in beautifully lithographed tin containers. Today's collecting market is reaping the harvest of the great tobacco tins that were produced. From the 1870s through the mid-1920s, manufacturers produced literally thousands of brands that were available in tin boxes of various sizes with captivating designs. By the mid-1920s, for the most part manufacturers turned to less expensive and ornate forms of packaging. The early tins were attractive and also served numerous utilitarian purposes. Many were saved over the years. I'm always impressed when I see a tobacco tin that has remained in very good condition for 70 to 100 years or more.

In today's collecting market, tobacco tins are the most sought after and collected category of tin container collecting. Some of the very desirable and scarce tobacco tins are demanding astounding prices if condition merits. It is often difficult to establish a fair price for scarce containers because they are not frequently offered for sale. When one does become available, the sky can be the limit as a result of the intensive demand. Fortunately, the collector has thousands of choices available and the demand for less than mint or near mint is sharply reduced as the condition of a specific tin goes from pristine condition downward.

In collecting circles, tobacco tins are generally assigned a condition rating on a scale of 1 through 10, with 10 being the favored condition. Few serious collectors are usually interested in any grade below 6. Condition is often described as Mint, Near Mint, Excellent/Fine, Good, or Fair/Poor. In the Excellent/Fine category, a discriminating collector may refine a rating further to Fine/Plus, Fine, and Fine/minus. I would also suggest that there is another category that requires consideration. With the amazing increases in reported prices, there is now a demand for having tins restored and there are tin restoration artists of various levels of ability offering to restore tobacco and other tins to original condition. We have now reached a point where Restored is a category that will demand some consideration. How will values be affected? Certainly minor restoration will be in a different category than major restoration. It will be up to dealers and the collecting market to eventually make a determination in this area. If one is about to make a major investment in a tin tobacco container, it is possible, with close examination, to determine if restoration has taken place.

Advertising of tobacco products expanded to incredible lengths. Colorful posters, tin signs, trade cards, and free premiums helped keep the general store's male customers coming with great haste to the tobacco counter. It was possible to own a mantle clock, a pistol, a razor, bars of soap, and a pocket watch if the customer could accumulate enough coupons. Competition was fierce. From 1896 through 1898, more than a fifth of the nation's plug tobacco was sold at a loss as a result of the numerous brands on the market seeking customers.

Interestingly, snuff was considered a proper tobacco form for women, and brands like Lady Belle and Egyptian Queen were widely used. It was thought to be indecent, however, for a lady to smoke cigars or use pipes. It is doubtful that a woman could have retained her self-respect in the years 1865 to 1915 if she had smoked either a cigarette or a cigar. But snuff seemed to be fine and many dozens of eggs were exchanged for it.

Accounts at stores were often settled with a free cigar provided by the storekeeper to show his appreciation. Companies were eager to offer free tobacco plug cutters to the general store proprietor with the hope that the company's goods would be favored. Others were purchased directly from companies like Enterprise.

The star of tobacco collectibles would be the wooden Indian. Although most of these figures appeared in tobacco stores, there is evidence of use by general stores to promote their tobacco trade. The use of wooden Indian trade figures continued into the twentieth century but by the 1920s their numbers had dwindled rapidly. It became no longer fashionable to use them and with increased populations, some town ordinances considered them to be a sidewalk obstruction and banned them. For years they served as silent salesmen in America. They were generally carved from white pine and finished in striking colors. Although the majority of the figures were Indians, there were baseball players, Turks, Punch figures, and others. The demand became so extensive after the Civil War that figures began to be manufactured in metal. The old-time woodcarvers could not supply the numbers requested. Cigar figures can range in value from the $7,500 to $25,000 range and far more. The quality, condition, and origin of a figure will affect value. Many more of these figures were thrown out, burned, vandalized or destroyed than survived. The better figures can command virtually any price.

Even in the era of popular and extensive tobacco usage, there was always a degree of sentiment against using tobacco products. Mark Twain, a devoted cigar and pipe smoker, said he could give up smoking with ease and had if fact done so "hundreds of times." There is a category of tobacco collectibles including various brands of tins and other containers

promoting a "cure" to stop smoking. No-To-Bac and Baco-Cure were two products available in the early 1900s. Baco-Curo claimed to be effective by "building up the system, enriching the blood, toning up the stomach, and increasing the appetite and digestive power." The product goes on to assert that it "cures the tobacco dyspepsia, makes weak and nervous men strong and vigorous and promotes sleep." One can only guess regarding the contents since the product pre-dated the Pure Food and Drug Act.

In 1860, $9 million worth of cigars were made for the market against $21 million worth of chewing and smoking tobacco. The tax revenue generated was substantial. The customer of tobacco found it economical to purchase plug tobacco by the pound at 25 cents and slice it into their pipes. The alternative was to pay 65 cents a pound for plug cut or a granulated mixture. In 1897, chewing tobacco accounted for half of all leaf used in manufacturing. Plug tobacco was made in rectangular slabs about 1" thick and could be cut in a length to satisfy the customer. The plug was scored for cutting into small chews.

Tin tags were included with plug tobacco as a trademark and some assurance of quality. Additionally, tags were redeemable for prizes and cash. As an example of the extent of this aspect of the business, in 1902 one manufacturer spent $1,567,000 in redeeming plug tags which was an amazing sum in the days when a dollar represented a substantial amount.

Tobacco smoke mingled with the other strong smells in the general store. It was customary to light up a pipe or cigar and engage in some spirited conversation. The one sale a store proprietor could count on was at the tobacco counter. Today's collectors are reaping the benefits of what is often called "America's first business." Tobacco was a traditional pleasure in the early days of America and served to contribute to an expanding economy. Everything from tobacco tins to cigar boxes are highly sought after. There are specialized collectors of pipe tobacco pocket tins, tobacco bags and cartons, posters, premiums, advertising signs, early cigar lighters, plug cutters, and store dispensers.

Years ago, I purchased a Pedro lunchbox tobacco tin. The container was in very good condition but what excited me most was the correspondence inside. Letters received from the early 1900s were carefully tied in ribbon and provided a wonderful feeling for life at that time in our history.

I feel there is much to be discovered in the tobacco collecting area. New finds continue to come on the market and prices for desirable items are escalating. The prices demanded for quality pocket tins can leave your head spinning. I have seen some private collections of tobacco material that would stand up well against the full-fledged general store stock of the 1900s. The condition of the collectibles was outstanding and the variety very extensive. I recently acquired a large Tiger Chewing Tobacco store container that still contained several packages of the 5 cent product. One can only guess why all the packages were not sold and how they were able to survive over the years. The smell of the product is still very strong.

Collecting tobacco tins and related items can be a very specialized hobby. Collectors may seek containers with specific illustrations, Indians and cowboys, horses, beautiful women, birds, distinguished gentlemen, wild animals, dogs, and political figures among others.

Collectors are now seeking cigarette-related material in growing numbers. The peak of chewing tobacco consumption in the United States was 1890. The amount was an astounding three pounds per capita. The year 1907 marked the peak of cigar consumption at 86 per capita. In 1913, the American blended cigarette evolved from pipe blends. By 1921, cigarettes became the leading form of tobacco consumption in America. Tobacco had become a billion-dollar industry by 1924. Cigarettes were considered fashionable and convenient. They were touted to have health benefits. Advertising took three steps forward and virtually every magazine contained ads for cigarettes. Cigarettes were added to the stock of general stores but pipes, chewing tobacco, and cigars continued to find favor in rural areas. This new product found a very expanded market. It was now fashionable for women to be seen smoking cigarettes. Smoking equality had arrived!

It appears that collecting tobacco memorabilia will continue to be a strong hobby. In view of recent historical developments in the tobacco industry and the demand that public places be smoke-free, the historical context of tobacco usage in America has created even more demand from collectors.

If the reader would like to learn more about collecting tobacco artifacts and the intriguing history of tobacco advertising, I would strongly recommend *Tobacco Advertising – The Great Seduction* by Gerard S. Petrone, M.D.

Betsy Ross 5 Cent Cigar. Self-framed tin sign. Simulated wood grain. $675.00 – 1,250.00.

Big Gun Chewing Tobacco. P. J. Sorg & Co. Middletown, Ohio. Paper. $275.00 – 475.00.

King Alfred Cigar lighter. $450.00 – 750.00.

Cigar Store Indian. Circa 1890. Original paint.
$8,500.00 – 14,000.00. Courtesy of Warp's Pioneer
Village

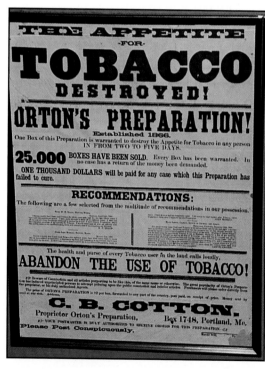

Orton's Preparation. C. B. Cotton, Portland,
Maine. Large poster advertising "The Appetite
for Tobacco Destroyed!" $220.00 – 325.00.

Helmar Turkish Cigarettes. Reverse wall-
mounted. Porcelain flange, die-cut.
$575.00 – 800.00.

North Pole Cut Plug Tobacco tin. United States Tobacco Co., Richmond. $135.00 – 250.00. Courtesy of Harvey Leventhal

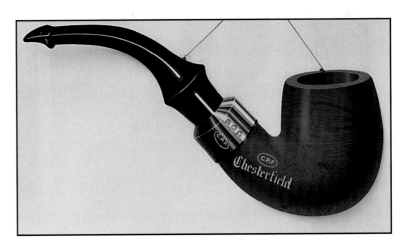

Chesterfield Pipe hanging sign. Die-cut. $450.00 – 650.00. Courtesy of Harvey Leventhal

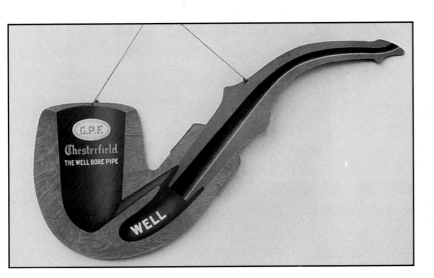

Opposite side of Chesterfield Pipe hanging sign showing pipe's interior.

Tennyson 5 Cent Cigar Counter display. Tin. $425.00 – 675.00. Courtesy of Harvey Leventhal

Blue Jay Tobacco. Orrison Cigar Co., Bethesda, Ohio. $135.00 – 175.00.

Three Hi-Plane Tobacco pocket tins. Left to right: $75.00 – 110.00; $80.00 – 135.00; $110.00 – 225.00.

Four tobacco pocket tins. Snap Shots Crushed Cubes, Falk Tobacco Co., $325.00 – 450.00; City Club Crushed Cubes, $150.00 – 200.00; Epicure Shredded Plug Tobacco, $150.00 – 200.00; Hindoo Granulated Plug Smoking Tobacco, $525.00 – 650.00. Courtesy of Harvey Leventhal

Taxi Crimp Cut Tobacco. $2,250.00 – 4,300.00.
Courtesy of Harvey Leventhal

122

Four tobacco pocket tins. Sweet Violet Cube Cut, $950.00 – 1,300.00; Hugh Campbell's Shag Smoking Tobacco, $175.00 – 350.00; Granger Rough Cut Pipe Tobacco, $475.00 – 850.00; King Edward Crimp Cut Smoking Tobacco, $275.00 – 450.00. Courtesy of Harvey Leventhal

Four tobacco pocket tins. Continental Cubes, $275.00 – 450.00; Golden Sceptre Burley Floss Cut, $175.00 – 225.00; Bagley's Burley Boy, $525.00 – 850.00; Three Feathers Plug Cut, $225.00 – 275.00. Courtesy of Harvey Leventhal

Four tobacco pocket tins. Bagley's Old Colony Smoking Tobacco, $85.00 – 135.00; Black & White Roll Cut Smoking Tobacco, $180.00 – 195.00; Guide Pipe & Cigarette Tobacco, $110.00 – 165.00; U. S. Marine Flake Cut, $120.00 – 180.00. Courtesy of Harvey Leventhal

Four tobacco pocket tins. Hand Made, Globe Tobacco Co., Detroit, Mich, $125.00 – 200.00; Grain Plug Cut, The Surbrug Co., $35.00 – 65.00; Vaporia Mixture, Falk Tobacco Co., $35.00 – 65.00; Bagdad Short Cut Smoking Tobacco, $85.00 – 110.00. Courtesy of Harvey Leventhal

Orchid Tobacco. $2,650.00 – 3,200.00.
Courtesy of Harvey Leventhal

Two Trout-Line Smoking Tobacco tins. Left: $375.00 – 450.00. Right:
$110.00 – 155.00. Courtesy of Harvey Leventhal

Lucky Strike Roll Cut Tobacco tin. $95.00 – 135.00. Courtesy of
Harvey Leventhal

Colonial Club 5 Cent Cigar advertising sign.
Paper. $225.00 – 375.00

Sure Shot Chewing Tobacco. Tin counter container. $475.00 – 625.00. Courtesy of Harvey Leventhall

Bull Durham standing bull. Bronze-like patina. Raised letters. $1,450.00 – 2,600.00. Courtesy of Harvey Leventhal

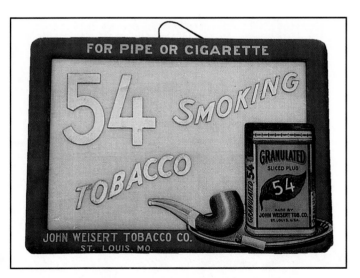

54 Smoking tobacco. John Weisert Tobacco Co., St. Louis, Mo. Hanging sign. $350.00 – 500.00. Courtesy of Harvey Leventhal

Tobacco tins. Orioles, $225.00 – 275.00; Flick and Floek, $325.00 – 425.00; Hi-Plane Tobacco, $75.00 – 135.00. Courtesy of Harvey Leventhal

Four tobacco tins. Beech-Nut, $110.00 – 150.00; Mapacuba, $65.00 – 125.00; Don Porto, $50.00 – 75.00; El Teano, $50.00 – 75.00. Courtesy of Harvey Leventhal

Tobacco tins. Sun-Kist Smoking Tobacco, $35.00 – 65.00; Even Steven, $75.00 – 125.00. Courtesy of Harvey Leventhal

Beech-Nut Chewing Tobacco display. $100.00 – 200.00. Courtesy of Harvey Leventhal

War Eagle Cigars. $65.00 – 85.00. Courtesy of Harvey Leventhal

*Scissors Cut Plug pocket tin. $2,650.00 –
3,200.00. Courtesy of Harvey Leventhal*

Tuxedo Tobacco tin sign. Embossed. $225.00 – 350.00. Courtesy of Harvey Leventhal

*Four tobacco pocket tins. Culture
Smoking Tobacco, $55.00 – 85.00; Four
Roses Smoking Tobacco, $275.00 – 350.00;
Gold Bond Plug Smoking Tobacco, $75.00
– 135.00; Coach and Four English Pipe
Blend, $115.00 – 175.00. Courtesy of Harvey
Leventhal*

*Four tobacco pocket tins. Eve Cube Cut,
$125.00 – 175.00; Maryland Club Mixture,
$150.00 – 225.00; Puritan Crushed Plug
Mixture, $125.00 – 175.00; Four Roses
Smoking Tobacco, $65.00 – 110.00. Courtesy of
Harvey Leventhal*

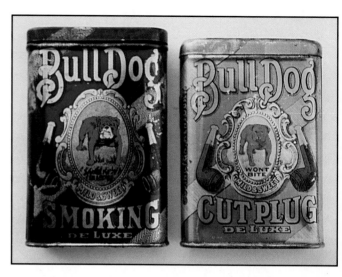

Two tobacco pocket tins. Left: Bull Dog Smoking Deluxe. $225.00 – 275.00. Right: Bull Dog Cut Plug Deluxe. $225.00 – 275.00. Courtesy of Harvey Leventhal

Four tobacco pocket tins. Full Dress Tobacco, $85.00 – 140.00; Totem Tobacco, $850.00 – 1,000.00; Matoaka Smoking Tobacco, $650.00 – 950.00; Trout-Line Smoking Tobacco, $135.00 – 175.00. Courtesy of Harvey Leventhal

Four pocket tobacco tins. Lucky Strike. $35.00 – 65.00. Courtesy of Harvey Leventhal

Four pocket tobacco tins. King George Cross Cut, $75.00 – 165.00; John Weisert's 54 Smoking Tobacco, $175.00 – 210.00; B. F. Gravely & Sons Special Pipe Tobacco Crimp Cut, $350.00 – 575.00; Crane's Private Mixture, $145.00 – 175.00. Courtesy of Harvey Leventhal

Four pocket tobacco tins. Cardinal Cut Plug, $950.00 – 1,375.00; Model Smoking Tobacco, $275.00 – 350.00; Lucky Strike Roll Cut Tobacco, $250.00 – 325.00; Full Dress Pipe and Cigarette Tobacco, $85.00 – 135.00. *Courtesy of Harvey Leventhal*

McCormick's Harvester Cigar box. $65.00 – 115.00. *Courtesy of Ken Kennedy*

Five pocket tobacco tins. Pinkussohn's Potpourri Smoking Tobacco, J. S. Pinkussohn's Company, Savannah, Ga., $75.00 – 100.00; Shot Crushed Plug Cut, $145.00 – 215.00; Tiger Bright Sweet Chewing Tobacco, $100.00 – 150.00; Mid-Channel Mixture, $125.00 – 200.00; White Manor Pipe Mixture, $120.00 – 180.00. *Courtesy of Harvey Leventhal*

Four pocket tobacco tins. Loving Cup, $1,000.00 – 1,450.00; Hi-Ho Smoking Mixture, $850.00 – 1,200.00; Checkers Tobacco, $250.00 – 425.00; Wagon Wheel, $325.00 – 400.00. *Courtesy of Harvey Leventhal*

Four pocket tobacco tins. Granulated Sliced Plug 54 Tobacco, $55.00 – 75.00; Full Dress, $100.00 – 150.00; Tucketts Abbey Pipe Tobacco, $75.00 – 135.00; Peachey Double Cut Tobacco, $55.00 – 75.00.
Courtesy of Harvey Leventhal

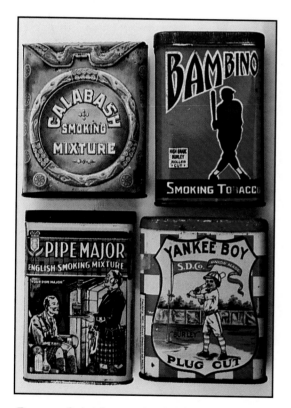

Four pocket tobacco tins. Calabash Smoking Mixture, $275.00 – 350.00; Bambino Smoking Tobacco, $1,000.00 – 1,400.00; Pipe Major English Smoking Mixture, $175.00 – 225.00; Yankee Boy Plug Cut, $425.00 – 550.00. Courtesy of Harvey Leventhal

Ten tobacco tins in display case. Peerless, F. F. Adams & Co., $65.00 – 95.00; Sweet Mist Chewing Tobacco, $145.00 – 190.00; Ojibwa Fine Cut Chewing Tobacco, $175.00 – 225.00; Union Workman, $45.00 – 80.00; Penns, $25.00 – 50.00; Old Rye, $40.00 – 75.00; Duco, $25.00 – 50.00; Eight Brothers, $60.00 – 80.00; Game Fine Cut (two illustrated), $425.00 – 600.00 each; Fry's Chocolate Case, $1,200.00 – $1,800.00. Courtesy of Harvey Leventhal

Four pocket tobacco tins. Honeymoon Tobacco. Left to right: $275.00 – 350.00; $75.00 – 135.00; $100.00 – 200.00; $75.00 – 100.00. Courtesy of Harvey Leventhal

Eight Brothers Long Cut Tobacco. Porcelain sign. 15" x 40". $675.00 – 1,100.00. Courtesy of Harvey Leventhal

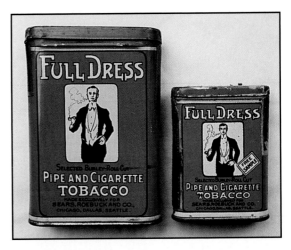

Two pocket tobacco tins. Full Dress Pipe and Cigarette Tobacco. Left to right: $100.00 – 150.00; $85.00 – 120.00. Courtesy of Harvey Leventhal

Hand-carved cigar counter clown with metal insert ash tray and papier-maché cigar. 21½". $1,000.00 – 1,500.00. Courtesy of Buffalo Bay Auction Co.

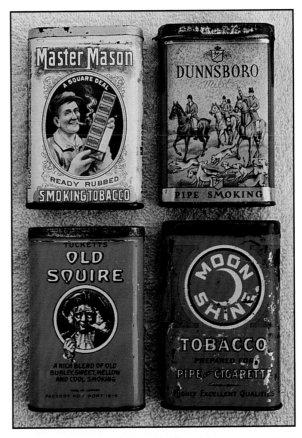

Four pocket tins. Master Mason Ready Rubbed Smoking Tobacco, $950.00 – 1,300.00. Dunnsboro Pipe Tobacco, $750.00 – 950.00; Old Squire, $125.00 – 165.00; Moon Shine, $375.00 – 600.00. Courtesy of Harvey Leventhal

Three Sweet Cuba Fine Cut store bins. Spaulding & Merrick Manufacturing. Chicago, Ill. Left to right: $115.00 – 135.00; $175.00 – 300.00; $140.00 – 250.00. *Courtesy of Harvey Leventhal*

Egyptienne "Straights" Cigarettes. Original frame. Cardboard. 21" x 30". $225.00 – 400.00.
Courtesy of Harvey Leventhal

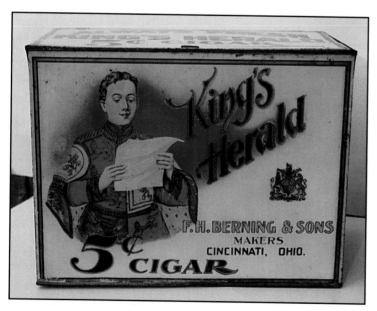

King's Herald 5 Cent Cigar tin store bin. $500.00 – 850.00. Courtesy of Harvey Leventhal

S. W. Venable & Co. Tobacco sign. Paperboard. 24" x 30". $550.00 – 875.00. Courtesy of Harvey Leventhal

Beech-Nut Store Bins with packages. Left to right: $150.00 – 250.00; $17.50 each; $175.00 – 275.00. Courtesy of Harvey Leventhal

U.S. Club House Cigars. Pennsylvania Cigar Corporation. $85.00 – 150.00

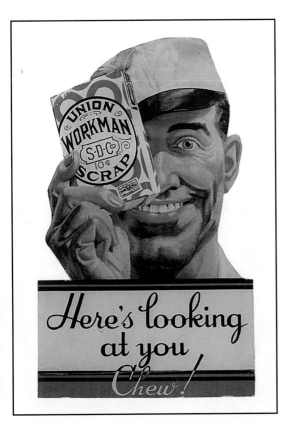

Union Workman Scrap. 22" x 14". Easel-back counter sign. $175.00 – 325.00. Courtesy of Buffalo Bay Auction Co.

Cowboy Cigar box. Circa 1886. $750.00 – 875.00. Courtesy of Buffalo Bay Auction Co.

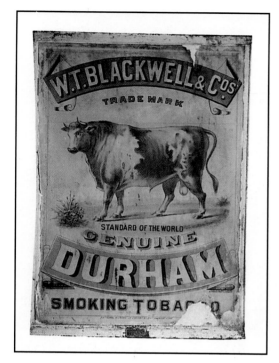

W. T. Blackwell & Co. Genuine Durham Smoking Tobacco. Store bin. $750.00 – 1,250.00. Courtesy of Buffalo Bay Auction Co.

Genuine Durham Smoking Tobacco. W. T. Blackwell & Co. Pocket tin. $165.00 – 225.00. Courtesy of Buffalo Bay Auction Co.

Large bust of Hiawatha. Circa 1900. 28½". $875.00 – 1,250.00. Wilson Collection

Three tobacco tins. Tango 3 for 5 Cents Stogies, $65.00 – 95.00; Option Cigars, $65.00 – 95.00; Three States Mixture, $35.00 – 65.00. Wilson Collection

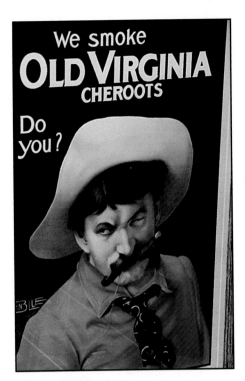

Old Virginia Cheroots. Advertising poster. $725.00 – 950.00.

Lorillard's Redicut Tobacco tin with bale handle. $145.00 – 225.00. Wilson Collection

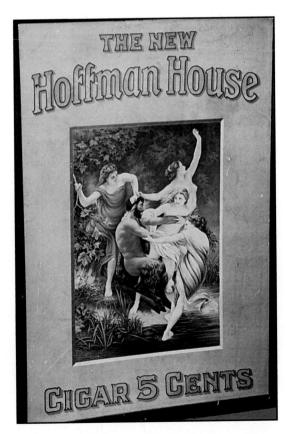

The New Hoffman House 5 Cent Cigar. Advertising poster. $375.00 – 500.00

Prince Albert "The National Joy Smoke." Paper advertising poster. $650.00 – 1,200.00. Wilson Collection

*Red Indian Cut Plug. Paper. 21" x 28". $500.00 –
800.00. Courtesy of Harvey Leventhal*

*Smoke "Nabob" Cigars. Paper. 14" x 18". $225.00
– 450.00. Wilson Collection*

*The Round-Up Cigar box label. $4.00 – 7.50. Wilson
Collection*

*Kennebec tin cigar box. Lithographs of American Indian on
top and inside of the lid. $155.00 – 285.00. Wilson Collection*

Overall view of Lorillard's Redicut Tobacco. $145.00 – 225.00. Wilson Collection

La Preferencia Seconds 5 Cent Straight Cigars. Paper. Artist proof. $375.00 – 650.00. Wilson Collection

Jack Rose Little Cigars. Paper. Artist proof. $350.00 – 550.00. Wilson Collection

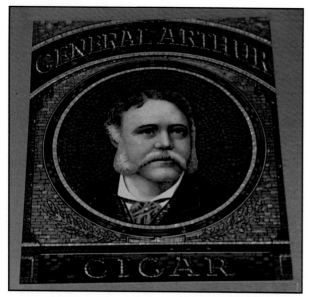

General Arthur Cigar. Heavy paperboard. Original frame. $375.00 – 600.00.

Country Merchant 5 Cent Cigar. Stewart & Holmes Drug Co., Distributors. 34" x 8'. Fabric banner. $2,500.00 – 3,200.00. Wilson Collection

Detail of the Country Merchant's face. Wilson Collection

Chapter Seven
·❖· BILLHEADS & OTHER STORE EPHEMERA ·❖·

The collector of old store billheads and ephemera can experience something that is quite unusual in the collecting field. A vast amount of such material is available at reasonable prices and much of it has not been discovered. The collector has the opportunity to seek it out and collect what is appealing.

A sharp eye and perseverance can lead to unlimited and exciting discoveries. Sources can be as close as your family members, old trunks and boxes, bookshops that deal in old paper items, print dealers, antique shops, garage sales, auctions, specialty antique paper shows, and estate sales. I have made some wonderful finds from these sources and others.

Webster's *New World Dictionary* defines ephemera as "printed matter (as theater programs, posters, guidebooks) meant to be of use for only a short period but preserved by collectors."

Old store billheads are very collectible on two fronts. The multiple designs of the letterheads are a testimony to the striking quality of early graphics. American eagles, early factories, buggies, firearms, tobacco products, patent medicines, historical sites, American Indians, whiskey, and beer are just a few of the subjects represented. Billheads are works of art that were custom-engraved for the storekeeper and his suppliers.

Additionally, early mercantile billheads often provide contents that are historically informative as well as a catalog of goods that were available in the nineteenth and early twentieth centuries. I have some in my collection that chronicle disputes between storekeepers and suppliers, the daily burdens of "keeping store," methods used to keep up profits, problems with shipments, negotiations with suppliers, concern about the coming of packaged goods, and timely payments of debts. Letterheads provide a true glimpse of that bygone era.

Trade cards, advertising material, posters, and other forms of mercantile paper can provide an endless range of collecting potential. Much of the material is presently inexpensive, but there are many items that carry impressive prices.

Some of the finest nineteenth and twentieth century lithography is represented in much of this material. The quality should not be surprising since much of the work was done by the very best artists and printmakers of the day.

I am always impressed with the great quantities and varieties produced. Hundreds of artists and printmakers devoted their working days to creating many remarkable items. Their imagination had no bounds and everything from the beautiful to the ridiculous found its way to an appreciative public.

The heyday of the trade card was from 1876 – 1900. These bright and colorful chromo-litho forms of advertising found strong favor, and manufacturers of virtually every product utilized them. Storekeepers often used stock images with the store's name imprinted. The store's name was also printed on product cards so customers could be ever mindful that items such as Kendall's Soapine, Agate Iron Ware, Clark's Mile-End Cotton, and Dr. Ayer's Cherry Pectoral were readily available at the local emporium.

Trade cards were produced by the thousands and were eagerly sought by store customers. They were collected and lovingly placed in albums to be enjoyed over and over. One printer of the day claimed that for $20 he could provide 10,000 trade cards imprinted with a firm's name and address.

Collectors should always be aware of the susceptibility to damage inherent in paper items. Transparent archival plastic sleeves that have no PVC and are acid free should be used to store a paper collection. Framing should be carefully done by a service that is familiar with the requirements of framing historical documents.

It is remarkable that so many early commercial paper items have survived the progression of years. Much of it was disposed of within a short period of time. Happily, there are still treasures out there awaiting discovery by the enthusiastic collector.

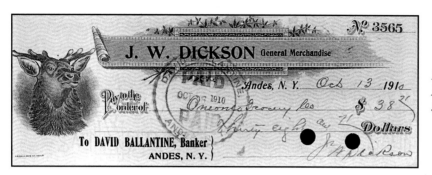

Illustrated check of J. W. Dickson, General Merchandise. Andes, New York. October 13, 1910. $3.00 – 7.00. Wilson Collection

Van Voorhies & Co. Saddles, Hardware, Harness, Leather, and other goods. Sacramento, California. June 17, 1918. $5.00 – 8.00. Wilson Collection

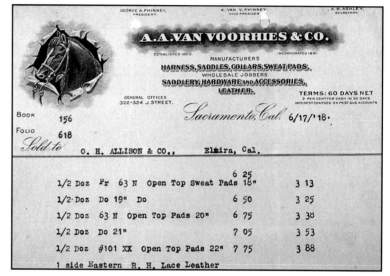

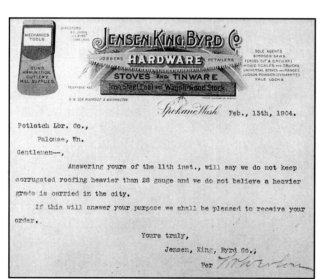

Jensen, King, Byrd Co., Hardware, Stoves, and Tinware. Spokane, Washington. February 13, 1904. $4.00 – 7.00. Wilson Collection

Oregon Condensed Milk Company. Hillsboro, Oregon. Unused check. Circa 1900. $4.00 – 6.00. Wilson Collection

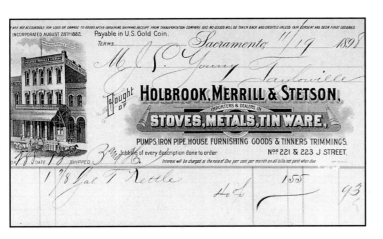

Holbrook, Merrill & Stetson, Stoves, Metals & Tin Ware. Sacramento, California. November 19, 1898. $5.00 – 8.00. *Wilson Collection*

A pamphlet poking fun at "Der Drummer." Drummers made the rounds of the crossroads general stores pushing their particular line of goods. They were always good for a joke and some news. $10.00 – 14.00. *Wilson Collection*

Colossal Storybook. McLoughlin Bros., New York. Striking cover of a plains Indian. Circa 1900. $75.00 – 125.00. *Wilson Collection*

The Child's Companion. Publisher not indicated. Circa 1890. Ads inside include Fry's Cocoa, Huntley & Palmers Breakfast Biscuits, and Wright's Coal Tar Soap. $23.00 – 32.00. *Wilson Collection*

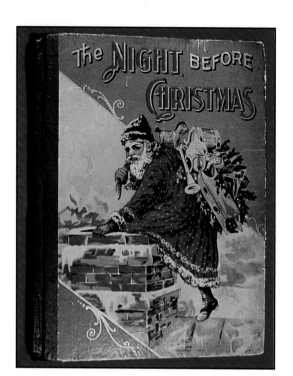

"*The Night Before Christmas.*" *Homewood Publishing Co., Chicago. Circa 1900. $45.00 – 65.00.* Wilson Collection

Unused label for Krout's Baking Powder. Albert Krout Co. Philadelphia. $18.00 – 26.00. Wilson Collection

A piece of "scrap" that was given out at Christmas to be enjoyed by young and old. $3.00 – 5.00. Wilson Collection

Little Chatterers. McLoughlin Brothers, New York. Circa 1900. $28.00 – 40.00. Wilson Collection

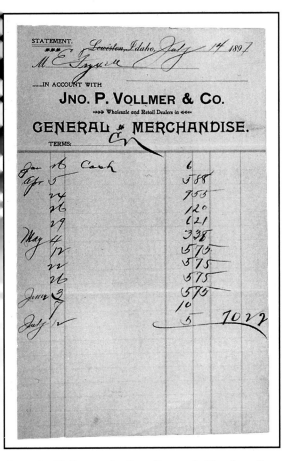

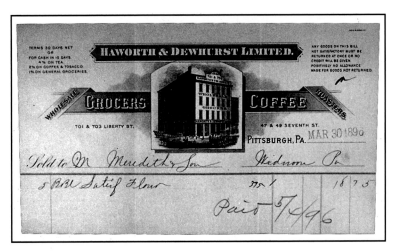

Jno. P. Vollmer & Co. General Merchandise. Lewiston, Idaho. July 14, 1897. $4.00 – 6.00. Wilson Collection

Haworth & Dewhurst Limited – Wholesale Grocers Coffee. Pittsburgh, Pa. March 30, 1898. $4.00 – 6.00. Wilson Collection

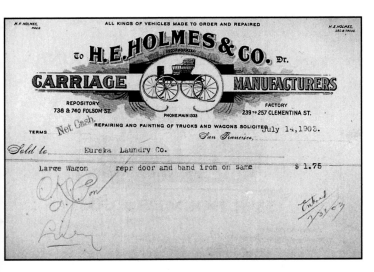

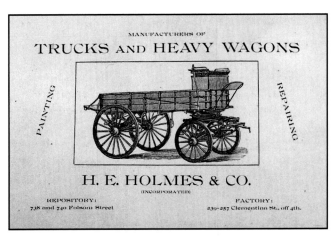

H. E. Holmes & Co., Carriage Manufacturers. San Francisco, California. July 14, 1903. Notes that the charge for the work on a large wagon to "repair door and band iron on same" was $1.75. $5.00 – 8.00. Wilson Collection

The reverse side of the invoice at left with an illustration of a large wagon. H. E. Holmes & Co.

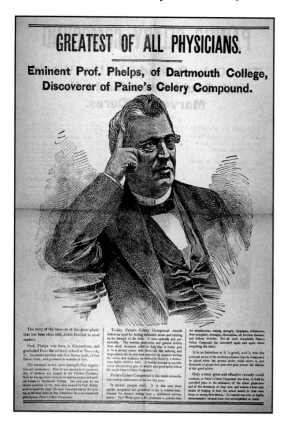

A typical handout advertising the many benefits of using Paine's Celery Compound. The discoverer of the product is illustrated. $9.00 – 14.00. Wilson Collection

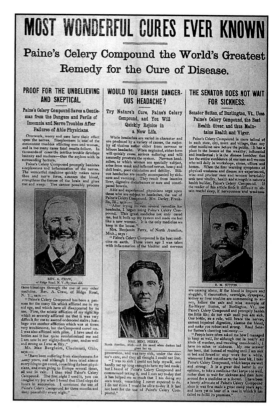

A page of the Paine's Celery Compound handout containing many testimonials with photographs

Kickapoo Oracle Indian Almanac, *1894. Great American Indian illustration. Handed out by the thousands to potential customers of this patent medicine remedy. $42.00 – 55.00. Wilson Collection*

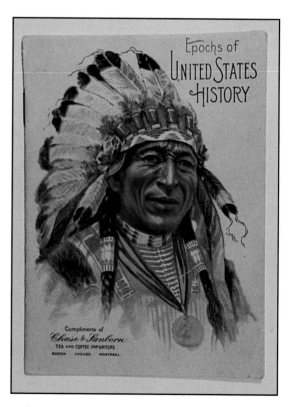

A handout from Chase & Sanborn, Tea & Coffee Importers. Appealing to children because it contained Epochs of United States History. *$18.00 – 32.00. Wilson Collection*

Unused label for Penrod June Peas. 1914 date on the label. Littlestown, Pa. $5.00 – 7.00. *Wilson Collection*

Unused label for L. J. Callanan's 43 Brand Sweet Corn. Oneida, New York. $5.00 – 7.00. *Wilson Collection*

Capitol Almanac for 1893. *Illustration of an American cowboy.* $22.00 – 35.00. *Wilson Collection*

Fold-out pamphlet for Dr. J. H. McLean's Liver & Kidney Balm. $35.00 – 45.00. *Wilson Collection*

Trade card. Perry Davis' Pain Killer. $4.00 – 7.00. Wilson Collection

Large trade card. Parker's Tonic. $6.00 – 8.00. Wilson Collection

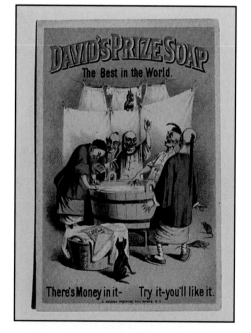

Trade card. David's Prize Soap. Illustration of a Chinese laundry. $7.00 – 12.00. Wilson Collection

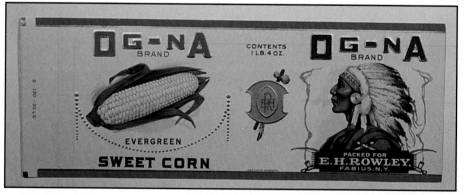

Og-Na Sweet Corn. Can label. Fabius, New York. $4.00 – 6.00. Wilson Collection

Squaw Choice Sifted Peas. Can label. Centerville, Md.
$5.00 – 8.00. Wilson Collection

Electric Tomatoes. Olney & Floyd.
Westernville, New York. Patented 1906.
$8.00 – 10.00. Wilson Collection

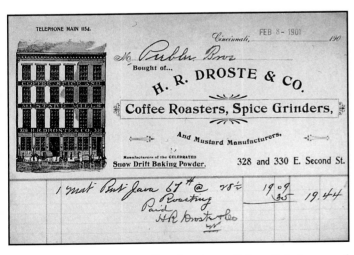

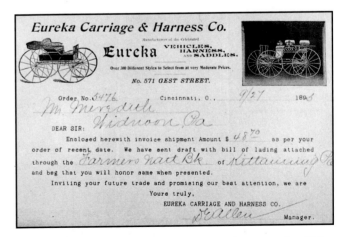

H. R. Droste & Co. Coffee Roasters, Spice Grinders, and
Mustard Manufacturers. Cincinnati, Ohio. February 8, 1901.
$5.00 – 8.00. Wilson Collection

Eureka Carriage & Harness Co. Cincinnati, Ohio.
September 17, 1895. Wilson Collection

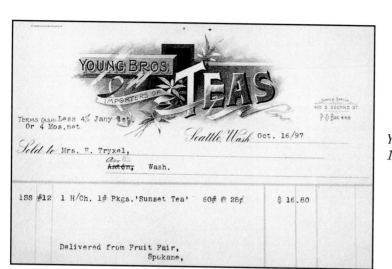

Young Brothers Teas. Seattle, Washington. October 16, 1897. $4.00 – 6.00. Wilson Collection

Washington Cracker Company. Spokane, Washington. December 17, 1891. $4.00 – 7.00. Wilson Collection

Forest City Red Pitted Cherries. Can label. Allen Bros. Co. Omaha, Nebraska. $3.00 – 6.00. Wilson Collection

Forest City Blackberries. Can label. Allen Bros. Co. Omaha, Nebraska. $3.00 – 6.00. Wilson Collection

Maryland Chief Beets. Can label. J. Langrall & Bro., Inc. Baltimore, Maryland. $4.00 – 8.00. Wilson Collection

Large advertising card courtesy of the Woolson Spice Company of Dayton, Ohio. The young girl is picking fruit. Copyright 1891. $8.00 – 14.00. Wilson Collection

Trade card. Hall's Vegetable Sicilian Hair Renewer. $4.00 – 8.00. *Courtesy of Ann Rooney Heuer*

Trade card. Mrs. Winslow's Soothing Syrup. $5.00 – 9.00. *Courtesy of Ann Rooney Heuer*

Trade card. Ayer's Hair Vigor. $4.00 – 6.00. *Courtesy of Ann Rooney Heuer*

Trade card. E. W. Hoyt & Co. Hoyt's German Cologne. Includes 1889 calendar. $5.00 – 9.00. *Courtesy of Ann Rooney Heuer*

Chapter Eight
❖ A VISIT WITH COLLECTORS & DEALERS ❖

When I meet a collector of old store material for the first time, it is always interesting to talk about what sparked the collecting interest. As you can imagine, the responses can vary to a considerable extent. I have also met spouses who share equal enthusiasm for the hobby and others that have no mutual interest.

The one common response is that there is "something" about early advertising and country store items that generates a great deal of interest. Superior graphics, a reminder of our past, colorful, and just plain interesting are comments frequently heard.

Spool cabinets, cash registers, spice containers, coffee grinders, seed boxes, and striking advertising can create considerable interest and dedication to collecting. A collector can also become very enthusiastic about tobacco tins or the elaborate spice, tea, and coffee bins that were produced in the late nineteenth and early twentieth centuries. Many of these were lithographed with illustrations of Oriental subjects, beautiful women, and children. Animals were also used.

I recall a trip I made through Colorado several years ago. It was easy to combine searching out old store items while enjoying the incredible mountain scenery. I made some good finds in Durango, Silverton, and Ouray while on my way to the Denver area. I had heard about a dealer that specialized in tin containers. When I arrived at his shop, he mentioned that his inventory was a bit low. He went on to say that a young lady had purchased a few candy and spice tins from him. A few days later, she came back with her husband to look at other tins that interested her. Her husband, a non-collector, started to examine the large inventory of tobacco tins and left three hours later after purchasing virtually every one. Another dedicated collector was born.

Over the years, I have met collectors and dealers throughout the United States and Canada. It seems that, in most cases, dealers that specialize in early advertising and country store items are also collectors. Dealing and collecting go hand in hand. The activity among dealers prior to the public opening of a major antique show is noteworthy.

My first exposure to old store material came through an ad in the local paper. I was collecting firearms and Old West memorabilia at the time but there was something intriguing about this particular ad. It had been placed by Chuck and Jennie Melville who were avid collectors as well as dealers. When I visited their home and viewed their collection and the items they had for sale, something clicked. I left with a Pratt's Vet Cabinet under one arm and a large bag in my hand. That was more than 25 years ago and I'm still purchasing items from Melville's Antiques. I was one excited person waiting for them to return from a buying trip. They became good friends as well as a great source for additions to my collection. Thank you again, Chuck and Jennie, for introducing me to such a fantastic hobby!

Ken Kennedy of Seattle, Washington, has been collecting advertising and store items for about 15 years. He feels there is a nostalgic appeal and is particularly pleased by the wonderful graphic qualities of the items that interest him. When asked what advice he had for both new and veteran collectors, Ken said, "buy what *you* like," and to the extent possible, buy items in quality condition. Ken became interested in spice tins about four or five years ago. He had a few spice tins that he picked up at various times and kept. Ken came to realize that there was an almost endless number of brands produced over the years, many of which were regional and distributed only over a small geographic are.

Unlike coffee tins, which were frequently emptied and often used for storage of everything from buttons to nails, spice tins had no secondary purpose so it is amazing that so many of them survived. I think one answer for that is that the contents of spice containers were frequently not completely used and, as a result, kept on hand in the pantry.

Ken told me that one noteworthy spice tin find was his first Imperial Brand from Spokane, Washington. Ken had a paper label Juno Brand (also from Spokane) which he had owned for a year or two and he noticed a small tear at the edge which revealed a lithographed tin surface underneath. As with most collectors, Ken's curiosity got the best of him and he carefully soaked the label off and was very pleasantly surprised to find a wonderful tin with an illustration of a train on a bridge.

Charlene Tsirigotis lives in Maryland and as long as she can remember has loved old general stores. She comments that she even married into a family that owned an old country store. She says that she was irresistibly drawn to collecting general store memorabilia, including advertising signs, tins, and boxes, She is now the proud owner of the Apple Basket Country Store in Mechanicsville, Maryland, a store filled with vintage memorabilia.

Charlene tells a fascinating story about how she came to buy her own authentic, two-story country store. She calls it a miracle. She says that she asked the owner if she would sell the building and was shocked when the owner replied that the night before she'd had a dream in which she asked God to send someone to buy the shop!

Charlene has been a dealer for 15 years. The store she purchased was constructed in the late 1800s and still contains original counters and shelves both upstairs and down. Charlene sells the candy that was popular during the turn of the century and is always "on the hunt" for neat tins, signs, and store displays. She does most of her buying in Virginia, Wisconsin, and Minnesota. The age-old question — what does one retain for his or her personal collection and what will be sold? Being the owner of an authentic general store has to be as good as it gets!

Peter and Cora Crandall of Eagle Point, Oregon, are the proud owners of the historic Butte Creek Mill. The water-powered grist mill has gained national recognition for its stoneground flours, stoneground meals, cereals, mixes, and rolled grains. Next to the mill is the couple's incredible collection of general store memorabilia. Called the Oregon General Store Museum, the building houses a jam-packed country store with a large number of very scarce and desirable items. Peter was fortunate to be able to purchase the foundation of the collection intact and has continued adding to it.

As with most collectors, Peter is captivated by the wonderful graphics and designs of country store collectibles. He is also intrigued by the stories behind the companies that provided products during the golden age of the general store. Many of the companies have passed from the scene, merged, or have been acquired by other companies, but many survive.

Sherwood, Oregon's old commercial area has a great look. It appears that time has passed by and you are in the 1930s to 1950s. Vince Harbick operates a large shop which always seems to have a find or two for the collector. Vince has a real eye for merchandise and is particularly fond of the graphics in early advertising. An incredible variety of merchandise has left his shop over the years. It is always a pleasure to drop by for a chat and listen to Vince's stories. Vince has the same complaint as most dealers. Good merchandise is difficult to come by and the costs continue to increase more so than in the past. Vince has been a good friend and has provided me with some terrific country store collectibles.

Jerry Knapp and his wife are good friends of Chuck and Jennie Melville and they often participate in antique shows together. Jerry and his wife are avid collectors and have some outstanding old store items. They continue to be on the lookout for additions to their collection and enjoy dealing in advertising and store-related items. Jerry does incredible restoration work on old scales and coffee grinders. The scales, finished in period colors, are particularly delightful.

I met Myron Huffman at the Indianapolis Advertising Show. I am always impressed by the quality and variety of his merchandise. So many tins in such great condition! Myron's specialty areas are antique advertising, country store, soda fountain, brewery, fixtures, cabinets, containers, trays, and historic or nostalgic items. I hope dealers like him are around for many more years.

Peter Lovejoy is one of those very special dealers with a real eye for advertising and general store collectibles. As I look around my study, I can spot several "remembrances" of Peter. A large Prince Albert Indian series advertising poster, a Redicut Tobacco tin lunch box, a Chase & Sanborn ad, a Humphreys' Specifics cabinet, and the list goes on. Peter is an active member of the Antique Advertising Association of America and enjoys meeting collectors and other dealers. I always look forward to some pleasant conversation with him as well as information about collecting trends and prices.

I'm happy to see a collector become excited about the purchase of a longed-for tin container with a level of excitement that equals another collector who may have just spent $5,000 on an advertising sign at auction.

Collectors of old store items can encompass a very broad range. I have been a guest in homes where virtually every wall is covered with incredible early advertising worth substantial sums. I have also been privileged to share some time in collectors' homes with modest collections. What truly excites me is that the enthusiasm can be equal. I feel that I have truly learned something from every collector and dealer that I have spoken with.

For a collector, finding an outstanding dealer who presents honest merchandise at fair prices is like finding a great automobile mechanic. Never let them get away!

I would like to conclude with a word about the money a collector may choose to spend for a particular item or items. Collecting can be very addictive. A collector may have only one chance to acquire a specific item and it can be very easy and tempting to exceed the budget. More than once, I have run across a highly desirable country store collectible that I just had to have. A quick look at my checkbook left me with a disappointed feeling. My mind immediately began to recall items in my collection that I would be willing to part with in order to make the purchase. In some cases, I was able to make a trade. Otherwise, an understanding dealer or fellow collector agreed to grant me some time to raise the necessary cash.

I have witnessed a collector agonizing over a potential purchase. It has happened to all of us. Walking down the aisle at a great antique show, you are suddenly confronted with a dye cupboard or great tobacco tin that has been something you have always wanted. First concern — what is the price? If in the realm of possibility, negotiations begin. The collector may plead his or her case with a spouse. Are payments over time okay? Can the expense be justified in view of day-to-day living expenses? As the thought process continues, another collector appears and begins to inquire about the item. It looks like it's time to come to a decision. I know collectors that will walk away from an item if it is priced $5 more than they are willing to pay. Other collectors will make the purchase at virtually any price if the desire and ability to own the item are strong enough.

Every collector will have his or her personal way of dealing with the spending issue. There is no single correct answer. A large number of collectors with whom I talk say that the hunting for and acquisition of a collectible can be more pleasurable than actual ownership.

In 1961, Laurence A. Johnson wrote *Over the Counter and On the Shelf – Country Storekeeping in America 1620 – 1929*. Mr. Johnson always wanted to be a storekeeper as a result of his experiences as a boy in a store at South Butler, New York. His chance came in 1906 when he was hired as a clerk at a store in Clyde, New York, at a wage of $6.00 a week. From those humble beginnings, Johnson Supermarkets resulted. He never lost his love of the old country store, and in 1940 he set up a replica of an old-time store at his supermarket.

After his retirement, his love of the old general store continued and he spent his spare time collecting old store items and assembling complete and authentic establishments for museums and restorations. His searches for memorabilia led to the discovery of old store account books, catalogs, and other historical documents that provide a true glimpse of the workings of the old country store.

Mr. Johnson certainly must qualify as one of the earliest collectors and dealers of old store items. For that, we owe him a lot of gratitude. It was not until the 1960s that early advertising and country store emerged as genuine collecting areas. Prior to that, much of this material was thrown out, damaged, and generally not considered to be of much value, either historically or financially.

Collectors and dealers, for the most part, have been responsible for preserving this wonderful heritage of America. As the values of various items increased, more items came to the collecting market and will continue to do so. New discoveries of old store material are becoming less common, but they are still being discovered. As much general store material as I have seen over the years, I'm constantly seeing or hearing about something new. I wish the very best for all collectors and dealers as they continue to support the advertising and general store collectibles field.

Peter Crandall of Eagle Point, Oregon, standing behind the counter of his fabulous general store.

Chuck & Jennie Melville make their home in California and helped start me on the long road of collecting country store memorabilia.

Chuck's workshop area and where he and Jennie sort their finds after a long trip to the Midwest or some distant point. I was fortunate to acquire the Snow Boy Washing Powder box at a show in Portland, Oregon.

Another photo of Chuck's workshop. What about that Woolson Spice Company cabinet?

Vince Harbick of Sherwood, Oregon. Vince is very proud of his shop and has reason to be. It is a true collector's shop with great things coming in all the time.

A Peerless Tobacco box, complete with packages, on the shelf of Vince's shop.

A variety of tins and toys in an early display cabinet at Vince's shop in Sherwood, Oregon.

Ken Kennedy of Seattle, Washington. Ken had just sold that great tobacco sign he is holding.

Ken has a real eye for quality tins!

A corner area containing a small portion of Ken's collection.

I'm always anxious to get to Ken's booth at shows. He has great merchandise.

Peter Lovejoy of The Blue Tiger. Peter makes his home in New Hampshire and always has a terrific booth at the Indianapolis Advertising Show as well as other locations.

Jerry Knapp of California. A serious country store collector and dealer. His booth is a "must-see" at the shows where he participates.

A collector's corner.

Collectors and dealers deserve a big "thank you" for continuing to seek out and preserve our heritage. Look at the quality of this early board game, "Puss in the Corner."

Myron Huffman from Indiana. There is never a shortage of quality tins and advertising when you visit Myron's booth at the Indianapolis Advertising Show.

Charlene Tsirigotis of Maryland standing in her country store shop.

Another view of Charlene's shop, the Apple Basket Country Store.

As one would expect, Charlene is a collector as well as a dealer. The counter in her kitchen is an original store counter that fits right in with her love of old country store material.

Chapter Nine
❖ SOME WORDS FOR COLLECTORS & ENTHUSIASTS ❖

Much like our rapidly changing technology, the collectibles area continues to evolve. With emerging web sites, auction notices, and other communications via the computer, the collector has a new world available — the world of instant communication and information.

it is now possible to "visit" an antique shop and view the merchandise, become aware of auction activity, use e-mail to "talk" with other collectors, make specific inquiries with dealers, and generally keep informed about what is going on in the collecting field. The possibilities appear to be endless.

In recent years, there has been a significant growth in specialty auctions both in person and by mail. Much of the very best merchandise in the area of early advertising and country store memorabilia is now being offered at auction or by competitive mail bid. Old collections are being broken up and, in general, the sellers are choosing to retain the services of an auctioneer rather than selling their collections by other means. Based on some of the recently reported auction prices, it is easy to understand why a collector may decide to go the auction route.

As with most things, the auction method of selling has a plus side and a negative side for the collector. On the plus side, a significant amount of high-quality merchandise is available at one time in one location. Well-prepared catalogs are also available with descriptions, photos, and ratings of the general condition of the items. A collector may have an opportunity to acquire something he or she thought would never be available. Those that have interests in special categories, such as tobacco, food products, whiskey and early drug items, may have a chance to acquire a long sought-after item to round out a collection. It can be exciting to review a catalog and look forward to an auction.

On the down side, it is my personal opinion that auctions, in some cases, have caused prices to escalate to the point that participants must now pay prices that do not appear realistic. Can the item purchased hold the price paid? In many cases, that has not been the case. I have spoken to collectors that have purchased high-quality advertising at auction and found that they incurred a significant loss a few years later when the item was again offered at auction.

In visiting antique shops, the collector is usually not competing with a large number of collectors for a specific item. At a specialty auction, that is not the case. Mailing lists are developed and when an auction of tobacco tins comes along, for example, the competition can be incredible. I recently purchased a tobacco tin at an antique mall shop. I paid $55.00 for it. Shortly before that, I received the results of a specialty tobacco tin auction. The same container in similar condition brought $185.00. What is the true value of the tin?

I recognize that much of the early advertising and country store items a collector could once find in a general antique shop are no more. Demand has created this situation. What a joy it was to walk into an antique shop when I started collecting and find quality tobacco tins for $5.00 to $8.00 and tin advertising signs for $20.00. Now it is possible to visit a high number of shops and find nothing in the advertising/country store category.

Which brings us back to specialty dealers and specialty auctions. I am excited by the quality of merchandise now being offered. I have expressed my sentiments regarding prices. The reality is that collectors actually set the prices by what they are willing to pay. At this time, it appears that collectors are prepared to pay what is necessary to acquire a desired item.

Along with increasing prices, other considerations have entered the picture. When an early advertising sign brought $25 to even $500, the collector could generally believe the item was never restored. There was simply no incentive to do so. That has changed. Great signs, both tin and paper, can bring thousands of dollars. I believe it is very worthwhile to preserve a scarce sign through the restoration process. I also believe that significant restoration should be noted and that the eventual purchaser should be aware of it.

It has been interesting to observe what has captured the interest of collectors over the years. Tin advertising signs, store fixtures, pocket tobacco tins, paperboard oatmeal containers, spice tins, brand names, key-wind coffee tins, and drug items have developed huge followings. Other items from the old general store also have their enthusiastic collectors.

As remarkable as it seems, there are still store collectibles available for just a few dollars. Some of these include billheads, trade cards, and the more common tin containers. There continues to be something to suit the interests and budgets of the collecting community.

The earliest country store price guide I have in my library dates from 1970. Some of the prices indicated at that time appear unbelievable. All items listed were for "very good condition."

Polar Bear Tobacco Dispenser, $50.00.
Dunlap's Seed Box with Colorful Paper Labels, $20.00 – 30.00.
Fancy Oak Tobacco Case W/Beveled Glass, $100.00.
Premier Jr. Ornate Design Cash Register 1900, $85.00.
Framed Ulmer's Heave Powders ad, $25.00.
Adams Chewing Gum Glass Counter Container, $15.00.
Clark's Oak 4-Drawer Spool Cabinet, $75.00.
Clark's Mile-End Spool Cotton Tin Sign, $18.00.
India Mills Pepper Store Container with Bengal Tiger paper label, $20.00.

Things have certainly come a long way. In the early days of store collecting, it was possible to be a collector just for the many pleasures it provided. I feel it is now very difficult not to think of the investment aspect of collecting in view of today's prices. There will come a time when a value is placed on a collection for sale for inheritance purposes and the collector would like to feel that values will be in line with prices paid.

I should point out that premium items are bringing the premium prices. Personally, I can live with some wear and tear and have never sought out mint or near-mint items since the number of such items is very small and the prices can be staggering.

For example, in 1967, Ernest L. Pettit's *The Book of Collectible Containers with Price Guide* was published. It illustrates a Tiger Chewing Tobacco Store container (11" high x 26" cir.) with hinged lid with a price range of $8.00 – 12.00. This beautiful container remains very popular in today's market. I recently purchased one for $155.00 showing some wear but in overall good condition. I have also seen one in mint condition with an asking price of $425.00. The collector must decide what is important regarding condition. One can argue that even at $425.00, the mint condition container will continue to escalate in price at a higher level than one in lesser condition.

I have also found it interesting to go to a large antique show and observe the movement of an item from dealer to dealer. At a recent show, I admired an Enterprise Coffee grinder which was in original condition with paint and decals intact and the brass eagle. I saw it just after the show opened with a price of $475.00. By noon, it was on another dealer's table with a price of $650.00. After I made a second round of the show, I saw it on another dealer's table with an asking price of $875.00. This is not unusual. The bottom line is that on any given day, an item is worth what a willing buyer decides to pay.

The ability to replicate an authentic turn-of-the-century general store is now out of the financial reach of most collectors. The collectors that I meet appear to be very satisfied to acquire a fine example of an advertising or store item when opportunity permits but their collecting has been reduced in scale as a result of the escalating prices.

My excitement in acquiring a new item for my collection, talking with collectors and dealers, viewing collections, attending shows, participating in auctions, and researching the old general mercantile stores and their place in America's past continues to grow.

Some of the finest people I have had the privilege to meet are collectors, enthusiasts, dealers, and auctioneers of old country store material. As always, I would enjoy hearing from those I have not had the opportunity to meet, as well as old friends.

It has been a genuine pleasure to bring this book to you. Peace, joy, and good health to you all. Thanks again for keeping the old general store lights bright.

Interior photo of the old-time general store in miniature. At Christmas we add a small Christmas tree by the stove and other holiday decorations. The neighborhood children always ask to see it "with the lights on" when they stop by for a visit. The author's mother has provided some additions. Wilson Collection

Exterior photo of hand-crafted general store. Note the bench and barrel on the porch and ads posted on the side. Done by a New York craftsman to display his collection of miniature old-store items. Circa 1940. $375.00 – 625.00. Wilson Collection

SS Hand Made Havana Filled tobacco sign. Paper on heavy paperboard. Beautiful young lady. Circa 1900. $250.00 – 375.00. Wilson Collection

Cherry-Rocher Liqueur. Hanging sign. Heavy paperboard. Dated 1934. $125.00 – 200.00. Wilson Collection

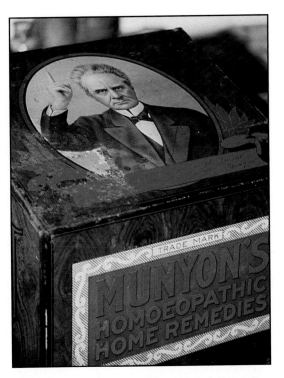

Snider's Catsup embossed tin sign. Circa 1910. $325.00 – 550.00. Courtesy of Buffalo Bay Auction Co.

Dr. Munyon's Homeopathic Home Remedies metal cabinet with contents. Very interesting graphics. $750.00 – 1,250.00. Courtesy of Peter Crandall

Exterior photo of an early Oregon general store. The "General Merchandise" lettering is still visible on the side. It appears much as it did in its glory years.

Gold Crumbs Tobacco sign. "Papa Likes Gold Crumbs Tobacco." F. R. Penn Tobacco Co., Reidsville, North Carolina. Embossed tin sign. $1,250.00 – 2,200.00. Courtesy of Ken Kennedy

Stewart Clipping Machine tin lithograph sign. 17½" x 15". $575.00 – 900.00. Courtesy of Buffalo Bay Trading Co.

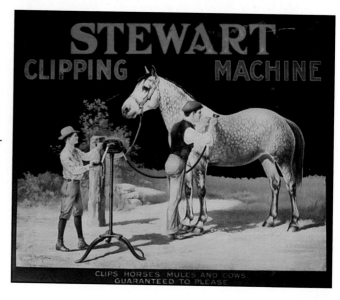

Large die-cut of beautiful girl holding a Christmas basket. Many stores would give such items to good customers during the holidays. $75.00 – 125.00. *Wilson Collection*

A pair of high-button shoes in very good condition. $85.00 – 125.00.

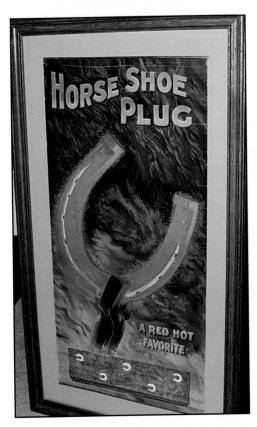

Horse Shoe Plug Tobacco. "A Red Hot Favorite." Large paper litho. Scarce. $400.00 – 650.00. *Wilson Collection*

Harmony Rose Glycerine Soap. "Makes You Feel As Fresh As a Rose." Large heavy paperboard advertising sign. Circa 1900. United Drug Co. $300.00 – 475.00. *Wilson Collection*

Interior scene of general store display. Burton, Ohio.

Exterior view of President Calvin Coolidge's father's general store in Plymouth Notch, Vermont.
Maintained as a historical site by the State of Vermont.

A "collector's corner." Wilson Collection

The side panel from an early delivery wagon. Paul and Pensyl. Very interesting letter. $2,500.00 – 3,850.00. Courtesy of Cary Station Antiques

Tip tray for Eye-Fix – The Great Eye Remedy. $375.00 – 550.00. Courtesy of Buffalo Bay Trading Co.

Great Majestic Ranges. Gesso base-relief store sign. 37" x 49" x 5" deep. Very scarce in this condition. $3,000.00 – 5,000.00. Courtesy of Buffalo Bay Trading Co.

A great collection of tobacco tins. Courtesy of Harvey Leventhal

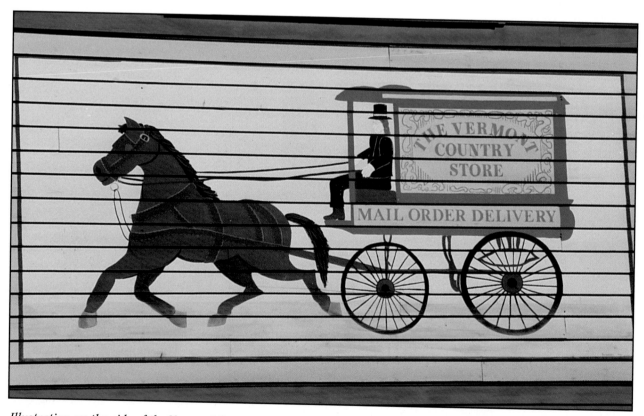

Illustration on the side of the Vermont Country Store of Weston, Vermont. A very interesting place to visit that combines modern marketing methods with old-fashioned service and quality goods.

Interior photo of the historical general store display.

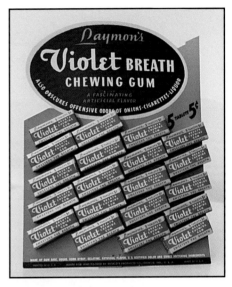

Laymon's Violet Breath Chewing Gum display card. Five tablets for five cents. $125.00 – 145.00. Courtesy of Harvey Leventhal

Gillette Blue Blades display. Circa 1940. Advocates the purchase of U. S. War Bonds & Stamps. $65.00 – 90.00. Courtesy of Harvey Leventhal

Ever-Ready Shaving Brushes, large and small boxes with brush. Grouping value: $75.00 – 115.00. Courtesy of Harvey Leventhal

Package of soap. Side panel states, "This soap is especially prepared for women who look after the care of their complexion." Queen Beauty Toilet Soap, Dr. J. B. Lynas & Son, Logansport, Indiana. $7.00 – 10.00. Wilson Collection

Kerr General Merchandise delivery wagon. Wisconsin. Wagons such as this one travelled the rural roads of America. Courtesy of Harold Warp's Pioneer Museum

Exterior photo of the Taylor Store, Ovina, Nebraska. It was available for the ranch hands and others in the area and also served as a post office. Courtesy of Stuhr Museum of the Pioneer, Grand Island, Nebraska.

··❖ BIBLIOGRAPHY ❖··

Atherton, Lewis. *Main Street on the Middle Border.* Bloomington, Indiana: Indiana University Press, 1954.

Bettman, Otto L. *The Good Old Days – They Were Terrible!* New York: Random House, 1974.

Carson, Gerald. *The Old Country Store.* New York: Oxford University Press, 1954.

Cheadle, Dave. *Victorian Trade Cards.* Paducah, Ky.: Collector Books, 1996.

Clark, Hyla M. *The Tin Can Book.* New York: New American Library, 1977.

Clark, Thomas D. *Pills, Petticoats & Plows: The Southern Country Store.* Norman, Oklahoma: University of Oklahoma Press, 1944 (Third printing 1989).

Dary, David. *Entrepreneurs of the Old West.* New York: Alfred A. Knopf, 1986.

Delo, David M. *Peddlers and Post Traders: The Army Sutler on the Frontier.* Salt Lake City: University of Utah Press, 1992.

Dodge, Fred. *Antique Tins.* Paducah, Ky.: Collector Books, 1995.

Grossholz, Roselyn. *The Collectible Classics From Commerce.* Erie, Pa.: self-published, 1978.

Grossholz, Roselyn. *Country Store Collectibles.* Des Moines, Iowa: Wallace-Homestead Book Co., 1972.

Harrison, Jim. *Country Stores.* Atlanta: Longstreet Press, 1993.

Heinmann, Robert K. *Tobacco & Americans.* New York: McGraw Hill Book Company, Inc., 1960.

Huxford, Bob and Sharon. *Collectible Advertising.* Paducah, Ky.: Collector Books, 1993.

Huxford, Bob and Sharon. *Collectible Advertising, Third Edition.* Paducah, Ky.: Collector Books, 1997.

Israel, Fred L., editor. *1897 Sears Roebuck Catalogue.* New York: Chelsea House Publishers, 1968.

Johnson, Laurence A. *Over the Counter and On the Shelf, Country Storekeeping in America, 1620 – 1920.* Rutland, Vermont: Charles E. Tuttle Company, Publishers, 1961.

Ketchum, William C. *The Catalog of American Collectibles.* Second Printing. New York: Mayflower Books, Inc., 1982.

Kovel, Ralph and Terry. *Kovels' Advertising Collectibles Price List.* First Edition. New York: Crown Publishers, Inc., 1966.

Lingeman, Richard. *Small Town America, A Narrative History, 1620 – The Present.* New York: G. P. Putnam's Sons, 1980.

Martin-Congdon, Douglas. *Tobacco Tins – A Collector's Guide.* Atglen, Pa.: Schiffer Publishing, Ltd., 1992.

Martin-Congdon, Douglas. *Country Store Antiques – From Cradles to Caskets.* Atglen, Pa.: Schiffer Publishing, Ltd., 1991.

Morykan, Dana Gehman and Harry L. Rinker. *Warman's Country Antiques & Collectibles.* Radnor, Pa.: Wallace-Homestead Book Company, 1996.

Needham, Walter and Barrows Mussey. *A Book of Country Things.* Brattleboro, Vermont: The Stephen Greene Press, 1965.

Petrone, Gerald S. *Tobacco Advertising, The Great Seduction.* Atglen, Pa.: Schiffer Publishing Ltd., 1996.

Pettit, Ernest L. *The Book of Collectible Tin Containers, Book I.* Manchester, Vermont: 1970: Forward's Color Productions, Inc., 1967.

Pettit, Ernest L. *The Book of Collectible Tin Containers, Book II.* Manchester, Vermont: 1970: Forward's Color Productions, Inc., 1967.

Raycraft, Don and Carol. *Book of Country.* Paducah, Ky.: Collector Books, 1986.

Rifkind, Carole. *Main Street: The Face of Urban America.* New York: Harper Colophon Books, 1997.

Roberts, Bruce and Roy Jones. *American Country Stores.* Chester, Connecticut: The Globe Pequot Press, 1991.

Ross, Pat. *Remembering Main Street, An American Album.* New York: Viking Studio Books.

Rowsome, Frank Jr. *They Laughed When I Sat Down: An Informal History of Advertising in Words and Pictures.* New York: Bonanza Books, 1959.

Sandler, Martin W. *This Was America.* Boston, Massachusetts: Little, Brown & Company, 1980.

Schroeder, Joseph J., editor. *Reproduction of the Sears Roebuck & Co. Catalog for Fall 1900.* Northfield, Illinois: Digest Books, 1970.

Smith, Elmer L. *The Country Store, The General Store of Yesterday.* Lebanon, Pennsylvania: Applied Arts Publishers, 1977.

Time Life Books. *This Fabulous Century 1870 – 1900.* New York: Time Life Publishing, 1970.

Time Life Books. *This Fabulous Century 1900 – 1910.* New York: Time Life Publishing, 1969.

Ward, Susan, and Christopher Pearce. *American Antiques and Collectibles.* Edison, New Jersey: Chartwell Books, 1996.

Wilson, Everett B. *Vanishing America.* New York: A. S. Barnes & Co., Inc., 1961.

COLLECTOR GROUPS, MAGAZINES & OTHER PUBLICATIONS OF INTEREST

There are a number of resources available to the collector and enthusiast that offer knowledge, the opportunity to meet others with similar interests, and some pleasant times. I have listed all those of which I am aware.

Antique Advertising Association of America
P. O. Box 1121
Morton Grove, Illinois 60053
Publication: *Past Times*

Tins and Signs
P. O. Box 440101
Aurora, Colorado 80044

Trade Card Collectors Association
Box 284
Marlton, New Jersey 08053

American Game Collectors Association
49 Brooks Avenue
Lewiston, Maine 04246

The Ephemera Society of America
P. O. Box 37
Schoharie, New York 12157

National Association of Paper &
   Advertising Collectors
P. O. Box 500
Mount Joy, Pennsylvania 17552
Publication: *P.A.C. (The Paper and
   Advertising Collector)*

Antique Review
P. O. Box 538
Worthington, Ohio 43085-0538

The Antique Trader Weekly
P. O. Box 1050
Dubuque, Iowa 52001-1050

Antiques & Auction News
P. O. Box 500
Mount Joy, Pennsylvania 17552

Mountain States Collector
P. O. Box 2525
Evergreen, Colorado

Collectors News & the Antique Reporter
P. O. Box 156
Grundy Center, Iowa 50638-0156

Midwest Antique & Collectible News
P. O. Box 529
Anna, Illinois 62906

Maine Antique Digest
P. O. Box 1429
Waldoboro, Maine 04572-1429

The Mid Atlantic Digest
P. O. Box 908
Henderson, North Carolina 27536

American Country Collectibles
GCR Publishing Group, Inc.
1700 Broadway
New York, New York 10019

HISTORICAL & OTHER STORES
THAT DEMAND A VISIT

The following list represents a very small number of museums, exhibits, shops, and working general stores that offer the store enthusiast the opportunity to visit and spend some very pleasant time.

Ancramdale General Store
Ancramdale, New York

Apple Basket Country Store
Mechanicsville, Maryland

Asa Knight Store
Old Sturbridge Village
Sturbridge, Massachusetts
(This interesting store was established in the 1830s and operated until 1863 and is part of a fabulous living history museum complex.)

California State Parks
Bodie Ghost Town
Bodie, California
(Early mining town that once had the reputation as the toughest town in the West. Includes an original general store containing old merchandise.)

Cass Country Store
Cass, West Virginia

Cheap John's Country Store
Waynesville, Ohio

Cumberland General Store
Crossville, Tennessee

El Dorado County Museum
Placerville, California

Fort Laramie Sutler's Store
Fort Laramie National Historic Site
Fort Laramie, Wyoming

Frisbee Store
Kittery Point, Maine

Grafton Village Store
Grafton, Vermont

Harold Warp Pioneer Village
Minden, Nebraska
(Fascinating complex includes The Peoples Store a complete old-time general store.)

Harrison Brothers Store
Huntsville, Alabama

H. N. Williams General Store
Dorset, Vermont

Hubbell Trading Post National Historic Site
Ganado, Arizona

J. J. Hapgood Store
Peru, Vermont

Knott's Berry Farm
Buena Park, California
(Located in Ghost Town.)

Living History Farms
Walnut Hills, Iowa
(The complex includes an 1870s general store with staff dressed in period costume.)

Lock Stock & Barrel
Ellington, New York

Mariposa Museum & History Center
Mariposa, California

Mast General Store
Valle Crucis, North Carolina

Milan Historical Museum
General Store Exhibit
Milan, Ohio

NcNeil Post Office & General Store
NcNeil, Texas

Newfane Country Store
Newfane, Vermont

Ohio State Historical Society & Museum
Columbus, Ohio

Oldest Store Museum in America
St. Augustine, Florida
(Authentic turn-of-the-century store museum
containing thousands of artifacts.)

Old Village Store
Bird-in-Hand, Pennsylvania

Petersham Country Store
Petersham, Massachusetts

River Junction Trade Co.
McGregor, Iowa

Roberts Mercantile Store
Elizabeth, West Virginia

Stuhr Museum of the Prairie Pioneer
Frontier General Store exhibit
Grand Island, Nebraska

Todd General Store
Todd, North Carolina

Vermont Country Store
Weston, Vermont

BUFFALO BAY AUCTION CO.

SPECIALIZING IN MAIL AND TELEPHONE ALL COLOR CATALOGUE ADVERTISING AUCTIONS (AUCTIONS ARE CONDUCTED QUARTERLY). OUR MAILING LIST CONSISTS OF DEDICATED COLLECTORS FROM ALL FIFTY STATES AND CANADA. IF YOU ARE INTERESTED IN EITHER CONSIGNING OR PARTICIPATING IN OUR AUCTIONS, GIVE US A CALL OR WRITE TO: BUFFALO BAY AUCTION CO.
5244 QUAM CIRCLE
ROGERS, MN 55374
Phone (612) 428-8480   Fax (612) 428-8879

Harvey's Antique Advertising

If you have been searching the net for a place to see vintage tins, antique advertising, and country store collectibles, this is the website location for you. Harvey Leventhal has developed a unique website that provides photos, facts, fun, items to purchase, and links to related sites.

Web address: http://www.antiqueadvertising.com

Another bestselling title from
David L. Wilson

Features an interesting text with more than 500 knock-out color photos of store fixtures, showcases, advertising items, patent medicines, dye cabinets, coffee mills, and much more. The historical text is paired with period photos of actual stores. A fascinating look at part of America's history and the resulting collectible field.

8½ x 11 • 192 Pgs. • HB • $24.95
#3819 • ISBN: 0-89145-588-4

COLLECTOR BOOKS
Informing Today's Collector
To order call toll free: 1-800-626-5420
7:00 am – 4:00 pm CST

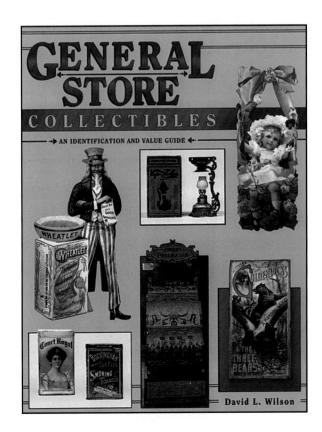

Schroeder's ANTIQUES Price Guide

. . . is the #1 best-selling antiques & collectibles value guide on the market today, and here's why . . .

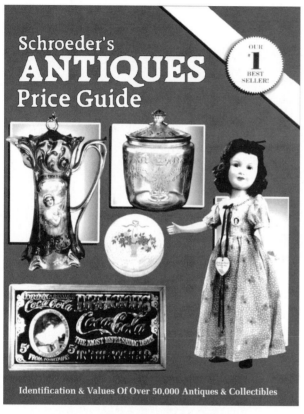

Schroeder's ANTIQUES Price Guide

OUR #1 BEST SELLER!

Identification & Values Of Over 50,000 Antiques & Collectibles

8½ x 11, 608 Pages, $12.95

• *More than 300 advisors, well-known dealers, and top-notch collectors work together with our editors to bring you accurate information regarding pricing and identification.*

• *More than 45,000 items in almost 500 categories are listed along with hundreds of sharp original photos that illustrate not only the rare and unusual, but the common, popular collectibles as well.*

• *Each large close-up shot shows important details clearly. Every subject is represented with histories and background information, a feature not found in any of our competitors' publications.*

• *Our editors keep abreast of newly developing trends, often adding several new categories a year as the need arises.*

If it merits the interest of today's collector, you'll find it in *Schroeder's*. And you can feel confident that the information we publish is up to date and accurate. Our advisors thoroughly check each category to spot inconsistencies, listings that may not be entirely reflective of market dealings, and lines too vague to be of merit. Only the best of the lot remains for publication.

Without doubt, you'll find
SCHROEDER'S ANTIQUES PRICE GUIDE
the only one to buy for
reliable information and values.

COLLECTOR BOOKS
A Division of Schroeder Publishing Co., Inc.